THE COMPLETE GUIDE TO
HUMAN BODY

PETER JONES

Sandy Creek
NEW YORK

CONTENTS

Words in **bold** are explained in the Glossary on pages 138 to 141

YOUR AMAZING BODY

Your body is amazing! Every day you use it for hundreds of different tasks—walking and talking, eating and sleeping, thinking and laughing. It works like an incredible machine, most of the time without you even noticing.

Millions of parts

Your body's machine has millions of parts. Each one is designed especially for the job it has to do. Lots of the parts work together so that you can, for example, eat and digest a meal, or think of a story and write it down.

You use your amazing body all day long to live an active life.

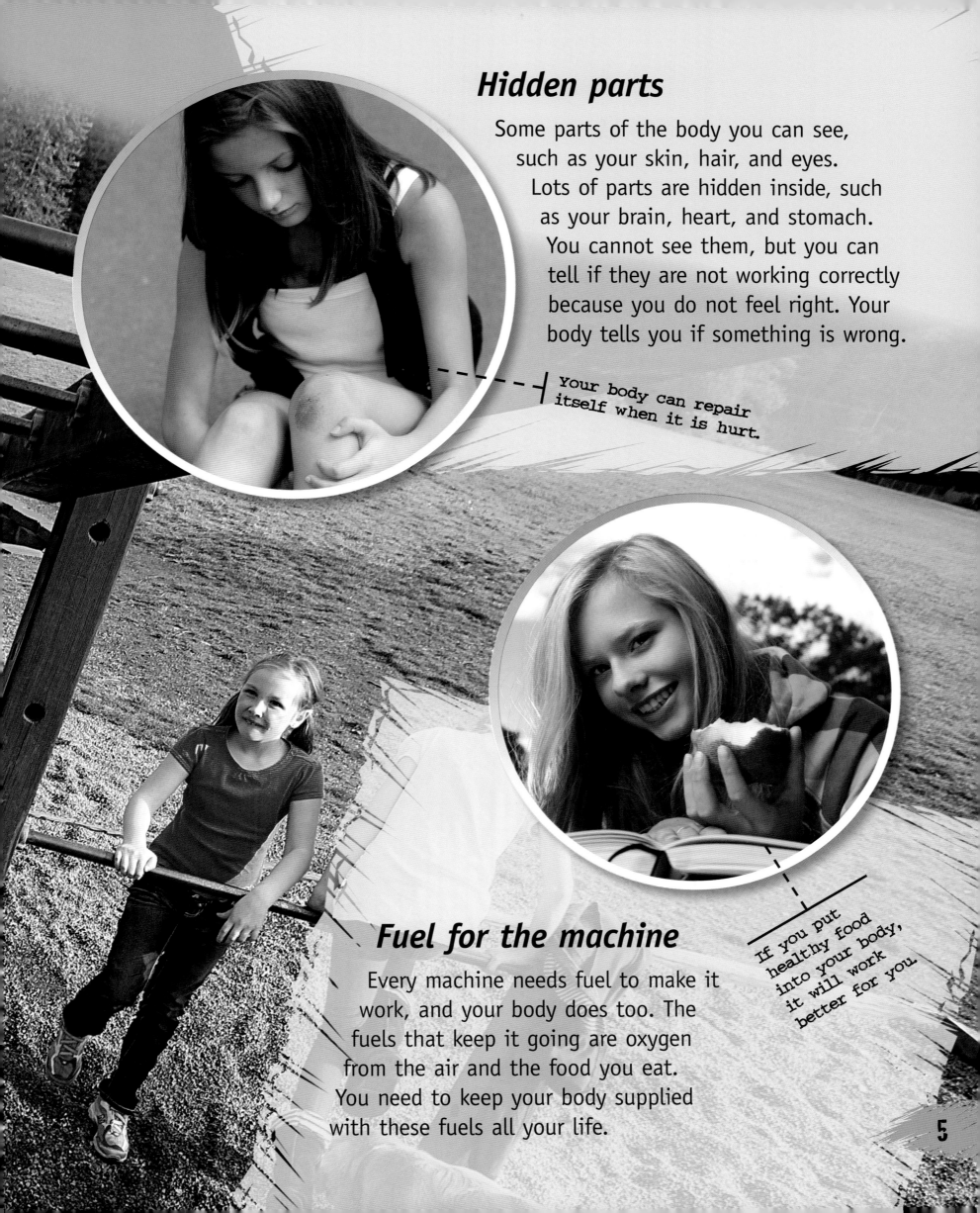

Hidden parts

Some parts of the body you can see, such as your skin, hair, and eyes. Lots of parts are hidden inside, such as your brain, heart, and stomach. You cannot see them, but you can tell if they are not working correctly because you do not feel right. Your body tells you if something is wrong.

Your body can repair itself when it is hurt.

Fuel for the machine

Every machine needs fuel to make it work, and your body does too. The fuels that keep it going are oxygen from the air and the food you eat. You need to keep your body supplied with these fuels all your life.

If you put healthy food into your body, it will work better for you.

SUPER SKIN

Your skin covers every bit of you. It protects your insides, it helps keep your body at the right temperature, and it sends messages to your brain about things you touch.

What is skin made of?

Your skin is the largest **organ** in your body. It has two layers. The top layer is called the **epidermis**. It is made up mainly of dead **cells**, which constantly flake off. The next layer is called the **dermis**. New cells from here replace the ones that fall off the epidermis. This layer also contains the nerve endings that **sense** touch. Below the dermis is a layer of fat that keeps you warm.

Hair

Dermis

Sweat pore   Dead cells   Blood vessel

Epidermis

Nerves

Fat

Every day you lose about 50 million dead skin cells from your epidermis.

Warm blood reaches your skin near to your heart more quickly than skin farther away. This is why your fingertips feel cold in winter.

Hot and cold

When you get hot, sweat comes out through tiny holes in your skin called **pores**. As the sweat dries, it cools down your body. You also look flushed when you are hot. This is because more blood is flowing through the skin, to lose some heat. When you get cold, the pores close and less blood flows through the skin. You may look paler.

Your skin sweats and looks flushed when you exercise. This is to cool your body down.

BODY FACT

By the time you are an adult, your skin will weigh about 11 pounds.

SKIN FOR YOU

Your skin is not the same all over your body. Its color, thickness, and surface pattern change on different parts of you.

Different colors

There are many different shades of skin color. A substance is in skin called melanin. The more melanin you have, the darker your skin color is. Melanin protects your skin from damage by the Sun. Everyone should protect their skin from the Sun by covering it with clothes and by applying sunscreen.

You see goosebumps on your skin when you are cold.

People with darker skin contain more melanin which protects them from sunburn.

Thick and thin

Your skin is not the same thickness all over. In some places it is very thin. On your eyelids, for example, it is only about a quarter of an inch thick. On the soles of your feet, it is ten times thicker.

Fingerprints

The skin on your fingertips has patterns of tiny loops and curves on it. These are your fingerprints. Everyone's fingerprints are different.

Your fingerprints can be used to identify you

HEAVENLY HAIR

BODY FACT

If you do not cut your hair, it will usually grow to about 40 inches long, then stop growing.

Hair is made of a substance called keratin, and it is growing all the time. Hair gives you warmth and protection.

What is hair made of?

Your hair is made of dead cells. It has no feeling, but your skin can sense movement if something touches the hairs on it. Hair can be many different colors. Its color is affected by how much melanin it contains.

Each hair grows out of the skin from a place in the dermis layer called a hair follicle.

10

How much hair?

On your head there are about 100,000 hairs. Each grows for about a year, then falls out and is replaced by a new one. There are about 5 million hairs on your body. They grow everywhere except on the palms of your hands and the bottoms of your feet.

What is hair for?

The hair on your head and your body keeps you warm. Your eyebrows and eyelashes protect your eyes by trapping dust and water.

Dark hair contains more melanin than fair hair.

Eyebrows and eyelashes protect your eyes.

BEAUTIFUL NAILS

Like your hair, your nails are made of keratin. Nails protect the ends of your fingers and toes. They can also be useful.

We use our nails to help with delicate tasks.

Growing nails

Like hair cells, nail cells are dead. Nails grow from under the skin at the ends of your fingers and toes. Fingernails grow almost 0.04 inches every week. They are useful when you want to grip and pick up small objects. Toenails grow more slowly.

Beautiful nails

It is important to keep your nails in good condition. If you do not cut your toenails, they can damage your toes. Some people like to decorate their nails or paint them with bright colors.

Nails can be painted to look attractive.

These are pieces of keratin seen through a microscope.

YOUR BODY OF BONES

Skull

Shoulder blade

Upper arm

Breast bone

Ribs

Lower arm

Spine

Your bones are joined together to form your skeleton. Your skeleton supports and protects you, and gives your body its shape.

Hundreds of bones

There are more than 200 bones in your body. Bones are hard on the outside, but inside there is a layer of softer bone. Some big bones have a tube through the middle, filled with soft bone marrow. When you are growing up, this is where new cells for your blood are made. As you get older, the marrow is replaced by fat.

Thigh bone

Shin bone

BODY FACT

The biggest bone in your body is your thigh bone, called the femur. The smallest is called the stapes. It is inside your ear.

Together the bones in your body make up your skeleton.

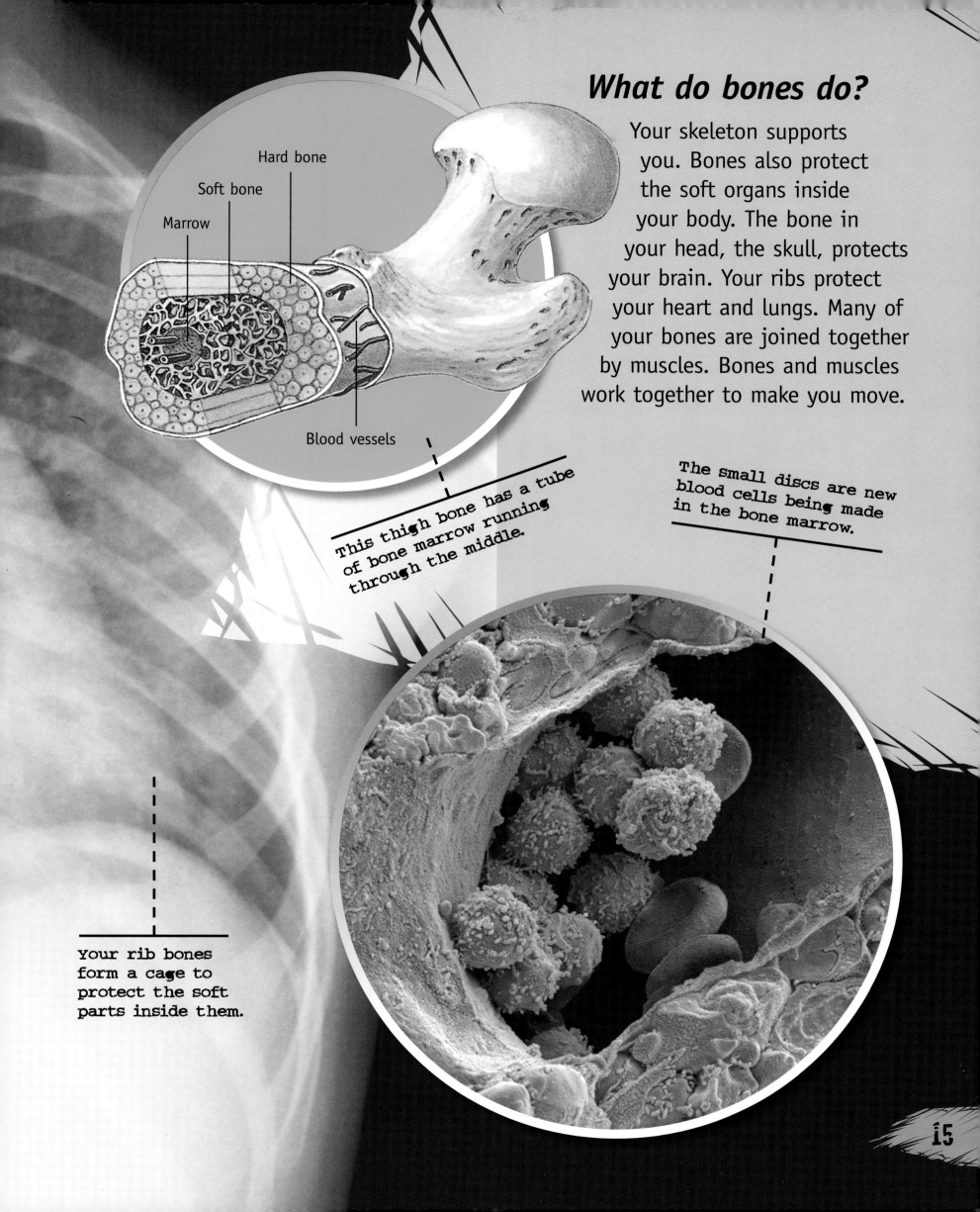

What do bones do?

Your skeleton supports you. Bones also protect the soft organs inside your body. The bone in your head, the skull, protects your brain. Your ribs protect your heart and lungs. Many of your bones are joined together by muscles. Bones and muscles work together to make you move.

Marrow

Soft bone

Hard bone

Blood vessels

This thigh bone has a tube of bone marrow running through the middle.

The small discs are new blood cells being made in the bone marrow.

Your rib bones form a cage to protect the soft parts inside them.

LOOKING AT BONES

Scientists have learned how to look inside our bodies at our bones, and how to mend them when they break.

Broken bones

If you break a bone, it can mend itself. It will make new bone at the place where it is broken. It needs to be kept still while this happens, so it may be set in a plaster cast. If the bone is badly broken, it may be held together with metal pins as well.

This X-ray shows the pins holding together a broken shin bone.

BODY FACT

Your body uses a substance called **calcium** to build strong bones. You get calcium by eating foods such as milk, cheese, and yogurt.

Looking at bones

For a long time it was impossible to see inside a living body without cutting it open. Then in 1895 scientists invented X-ray machines. These can take pictures of the inside of the body and show if any of its bones are broken.

Your big toe has two bones and the other toes have three each. The third bones at the tips are very small.

Eating yogurt gives you calcium to help make your bones strong.

Bony hands and feet

More than half of the bones in your body are in your hands and feet! Each hand has 27 bones and each foot has 26. Having this many bones makes your hands and feet very flexible and useful.

TERRIFIC TEETH

Your teeth help you chew the food you eat. They also give your face shape, and help you talk.

How many teeth?

Adults usually have 32 teeth, 16 on the top row, and 16 on the bottom row. Babies start to grow teeth when they are about six months old. By the age of five, children have a set of 20 teeth, called milk teeth. These are smaller than adult teeth. Each one will be replaced by a new, adult tooth. Most of your adult teeth will have appeared by the time you are 20 years old.

BODY FACT

The enamel on your teeth is the hardest thing in the whole of your body!

Milk teeth begin to fall out when a child is six years old

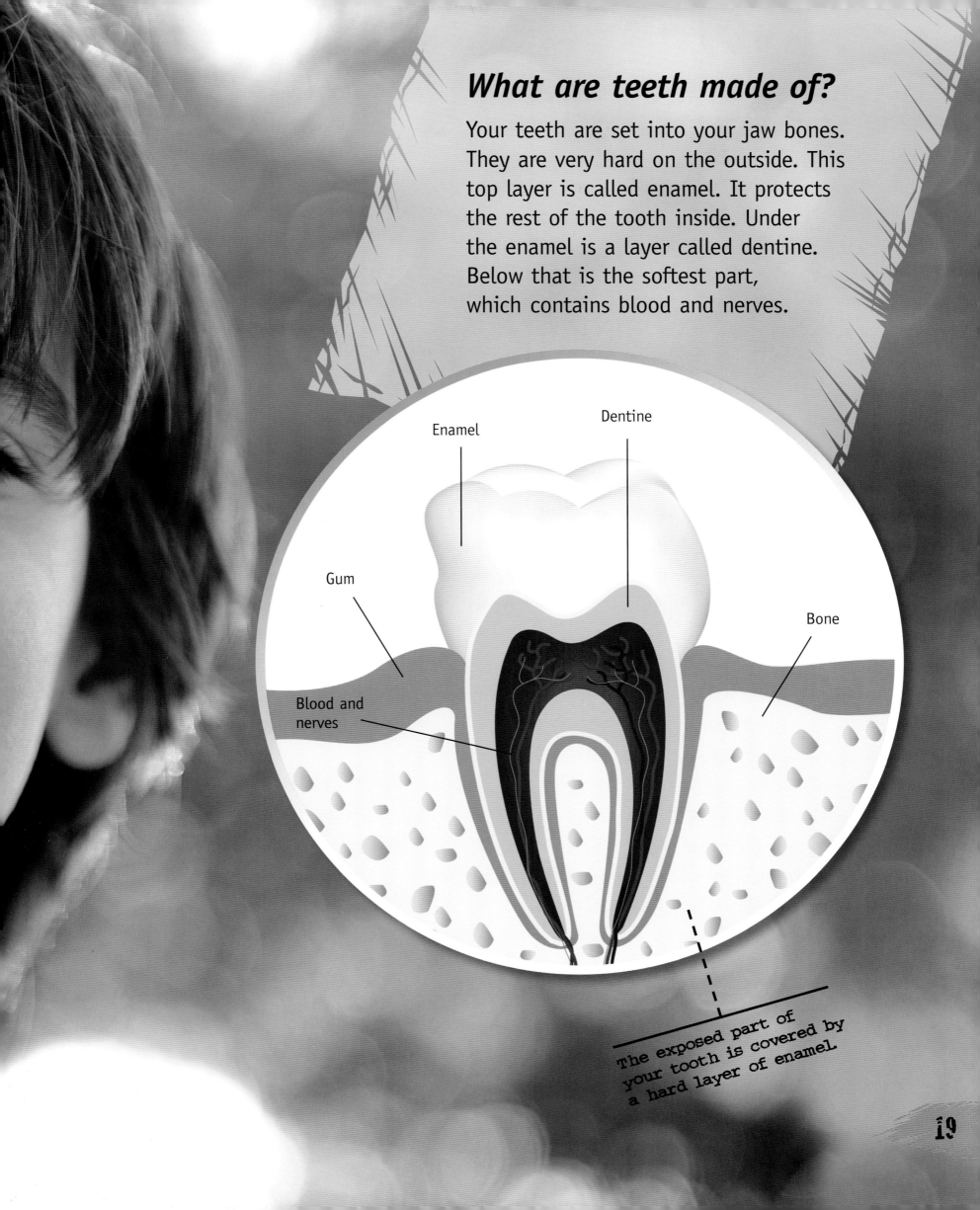

What are teeth made of?

Your teeth are set into your jaw bones. They are very hard on the outside. This top layer is called enamel. It protects the rest of the tooth inside. Under the enamel is a layer called dentine. Below that is the softest part, which contains blood and nerves.

Enamel

Dentine

Gum

Bone

Blood and nerves

The exposed part of your tooth is covered by a hard layer of enamel

PRECIOUS TEETH

Your teeth are amazingly designed. They come in different shapes, to suit the different jobs they do.

BODY FACT

Without our teeth, we would not be able to eat solid food. We would only be able to drink liquids, such as fruit juice.

You have differently shaped teeth for biting, tearing, crushing, and grinding your food.

Teeth for cutting

Your teeth are not all the same shape. The ones at the front of your mouth are sharper, good for cutting and tearing food when you bite into it. The flat teeth at the very front are called incisors. The sharp, pointed ones beside them are called canines.

Wearing braces can straighten your teeth.

Teeth for grinding

The teeth at the back of your mouth are bigger and flatter. They are good for grinding food into small pieces, so that you can swallow it easily. These teeth are called molars.

Molar teeth are flat on top. They grind food between the top and bottom rows.

JOINTS FOR JUMPING

Joints are the places where your bones meet and join. Different kinds of joints move in different ways.

Joining the bones

The bones in a joint are held together by strong cords called ligaments. The ends of the bones are coated with a smooth substance called cartilage. This makes it easier for them to move over each other. The cartilage is surrounded by fluid. This also makes movement easier.

BODY FACT

You can keep your joints flexible and stay fit by doing plenty of exercise all through your life.

In the knee joint, there are ligaments at the front and the back that hold the bones together.

Bone

Ligament

Fluid

Cartilage

Bone

The ball and socket hip joint makes movement possible in any direction.

Hip joint

Joints of different shapes give different kinds of movement. The joint at your hip allows you to move your leg around in any direction. This is called a ball and socket joint, because a ball shape at the top of your leg bone fits into the cup shape in your hip bone.

23

JOINTS ALL OVER

Some joints in the body can move more than others. Joints that move less are more useful for support

Elbow joint

The joint at your elbow allows a swinging movement backwards and forwards, but not around and around. This is called a hinge joint, because it moves like a door hinge.

Hinge joints move backwards and forwards.

BODY FACT

Girls are more flexible than boys because their joints move more.

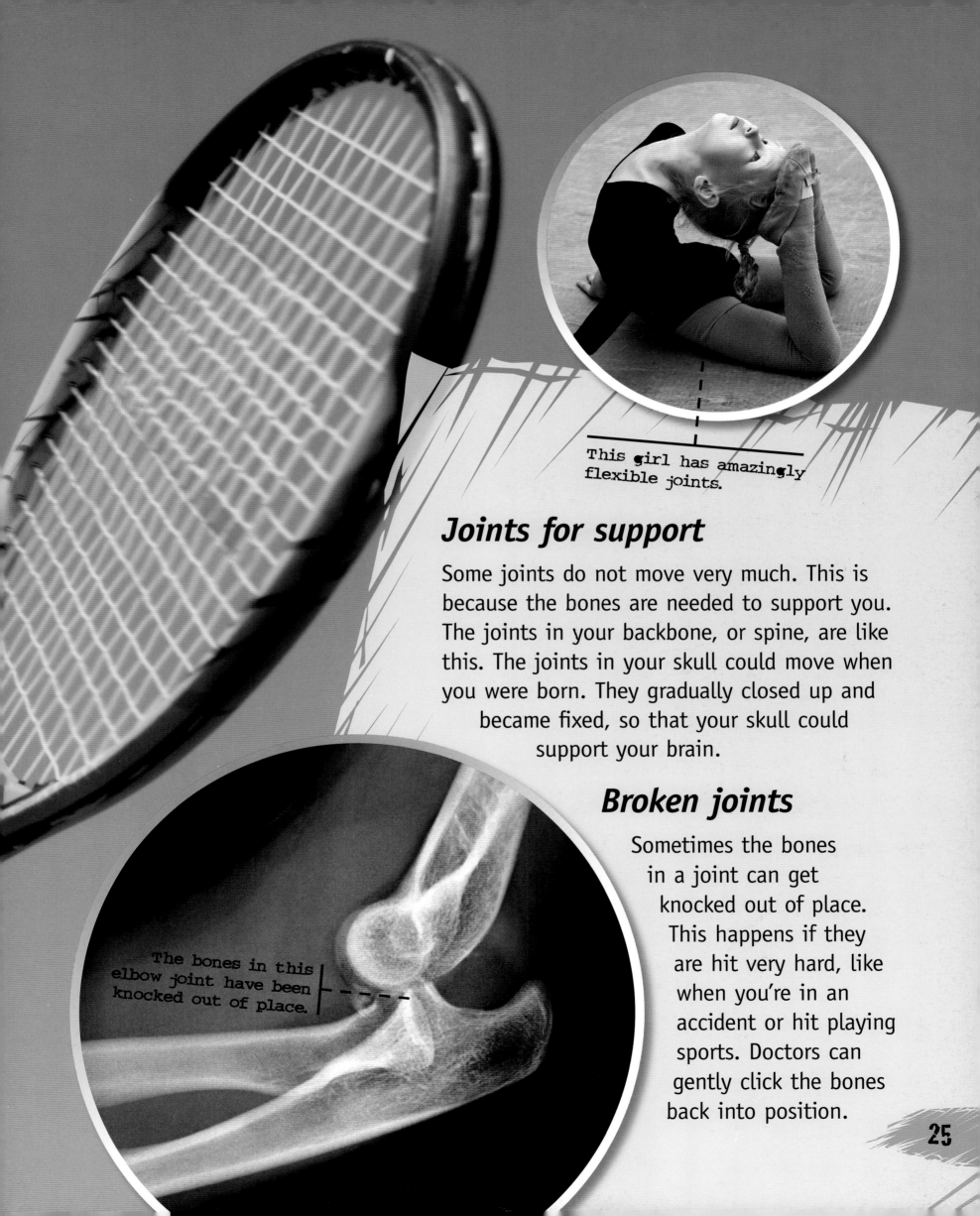

This girl has amazingly flexible joints.

Joints for support

Some joints do not move very much. This is because the bones are needed to support you. The joints in your backbone, or spine, are like this. The joints in your skull could move when you were born. They gradually closed up and became fixed, so that your skull could support your brain.

Broken joints

Sometimes the bones in a joint can get knocked out of place. This happens if they are hit very hard, like when you're in an accident or hit playing sports. Doctors can gently click the bones back into position.

The bones in this elbow joint have been knocked out of place.

25

MUSCLES FOR MOVING

Muscles work to make you move. There are hundreds of muscles in your body, allowing you to do lots of different things, such as walking and talking, even breathing!

Fleshy red muscles cover the skeleton, helping to give the body its shape.

Where are my muscles?

There are muscles in all parts of your body. The most important muscle is your heart, which pumps blood around your body. Other muscles are in your organs. These muscles work without you knowing it, for example pushing food through your **digestive system**. The third kind of muscle makes your bones move.

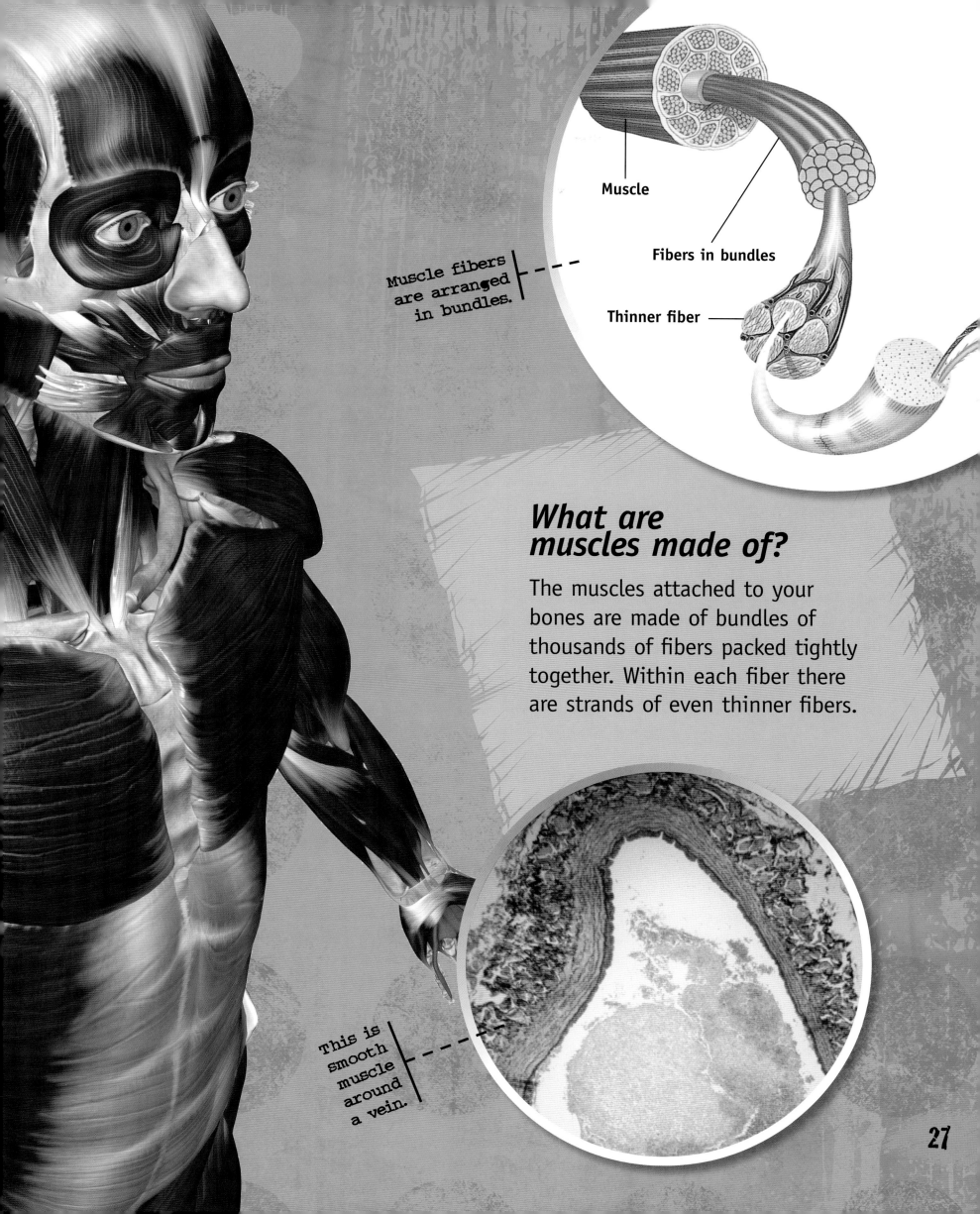

Muscle

Fibers in bundles

Thinner fiber

Muscle fibers are arranged in bundles.

What are muscles made of?

The muscles attached to your bones are made of bundles of thousands of fibers packed tightly together. Within each fiber there are strands of even thinner fibers.

This is smooth muscle around a vein.

MIGHTY MUSCLES

Muscles work in pairs to make you move. You can exercise to make your muscles big and strong.

How do muscles work?

Muscles can only pull. They cannot push. They work in pairs. When one muscle tightens, the opposite muscle relaxes. The tightened muscle pulls the bone it is attached to. The muscle on the other side of the bone relaxes and gets longer.

The muscles in your arms work together all the time.

Biceps muscle tightens

Triceps muscle relaxes

Biceps muscle relaxes

Triceps muscle tightens

Strong muscles

Muscles that are exercised regularly will become bigger and stronger. If you do not use your muscles by keeping active, they will become weak. Before doing any exercise, it is important to warm up your muscles so that they are not injured.

We use our face muscles to show each other our feelings.

Face muscles

There are lots of muscles in your face. You use them to show all your feelings, such as when you are happy, sad, worried, scared, or angry. More muscles are used to frown than to smile.

People who do sports work hard to build strength in their muscles.

BODY FACT

A muscle moves when all the thin fibers inside it contract (or become shorter) together.

A BODY FULL OF ORGANS

Each organ in your body does a particular job. Some organs work together, others work on their own. Together they form an amazing instrument.

Organs in your body

Most of your organs are packed tightly in the central part of your body. Your heart and lungs and the organs of your digestive system are here. Here also are the organs that remove waste from your body, such as your kidneys and bladder.

BODY FACT

Your kidneys remove waste substances from your blood. These leave your body in your pee, or *urine*, which moves into your bladder.

Tubes carry urine from your kidneys (top) to your bladder (bottom).

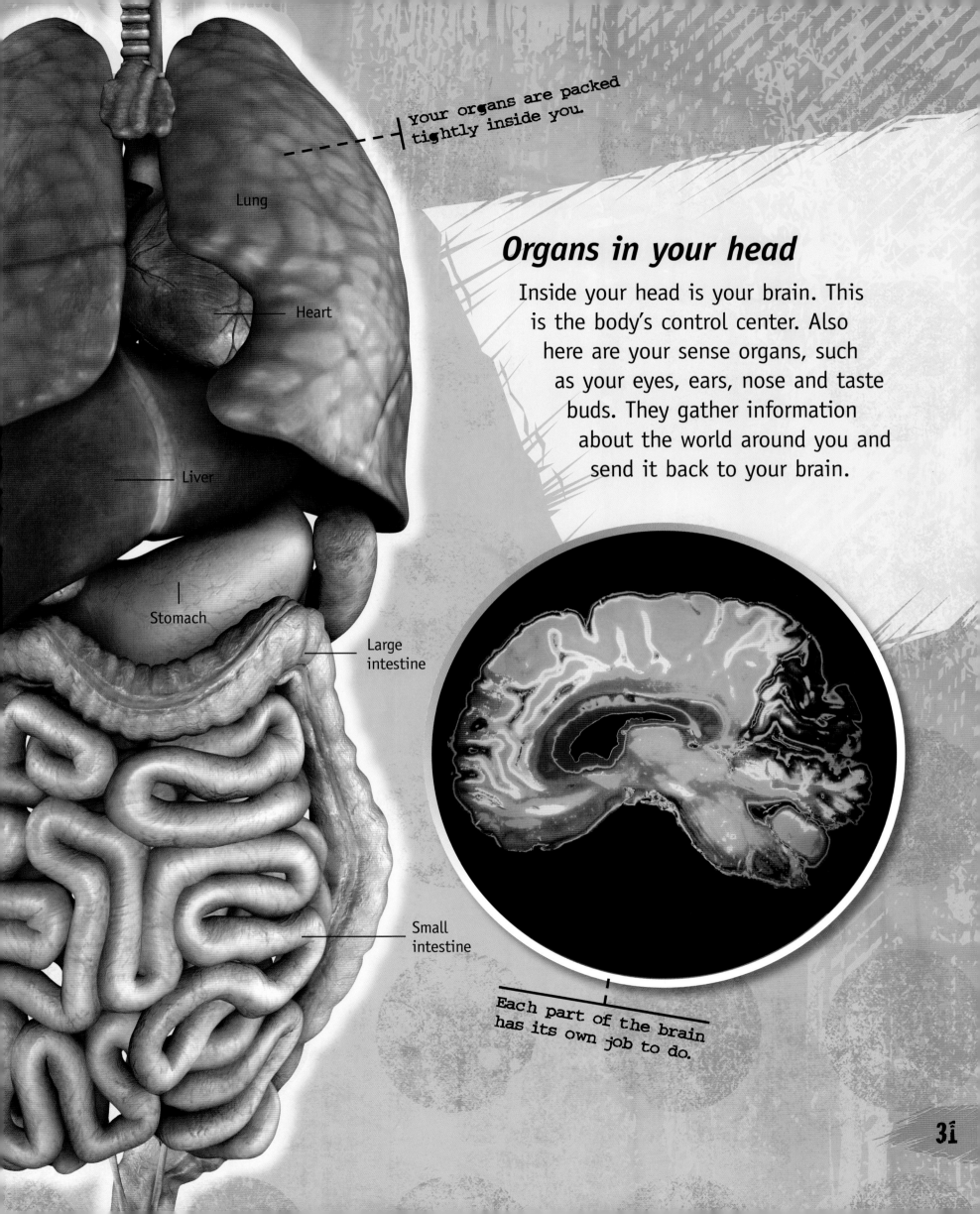

Lung

Heart

Liver

Stomach

Large intestine

Small intestine

Your organs are packed tightly inside you.

Organs in your head

Inside your head is your brain. This is the body's control center. Also here are your sense organs, such as your eyes, ears, nose and taste buds. They gather information about the world around you and send it back to your brain.

Each part of the brain has its own job to do.

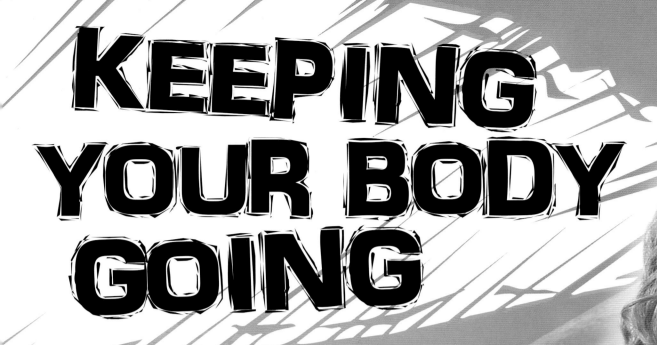

KEEPING YOUR BODY GOING

Your body needs fuel to keep it going. These fuels come from the air you breathe and the food you eat. They have to be taken to all parts of your body.

What is the circulation?

All the supplies your body needs are carried around in your blood. Blood travels through a network of blood vessels to reach every part of your body. Your heart is like a pump inside your body that pushes the blood around. This constant movement of blood is known as your circulation.

The transport system

Blood picks up oxygen from your lungs from the air you breathe into them. It travels to the heart and is pumped around your body in large blood vessels called arteries. Blood that is carrying waste products back to the heart travels in blood vessels called veins. It takes just one minute for blood to travel from your heart to your feet and back again.

These red blood cells are traveling through a small blood vessel

BODY FACT

If all your blood vessels were laid end to end, they would stretch around the world twice!

Blood circulates around your body through arteries (red) and veins (blue).

CIRCULATION AT WORK

The engine of your circulation is your heart. It pumps blood throughout your body, taking supplies to the parts that need them the most.

How does circulation work inside you?

One side of your heart pumps blood to your lungs to get oxygen. The other side of your heart pumps blood from the lungs to the rest of your body. When you exercise, more blood goes to your muscles and skin. This makes them hotter. When you rest, your circulation slows down.

This picture shows the heat given off by a person's body during exercise. The red and yellow areas are the hottest.

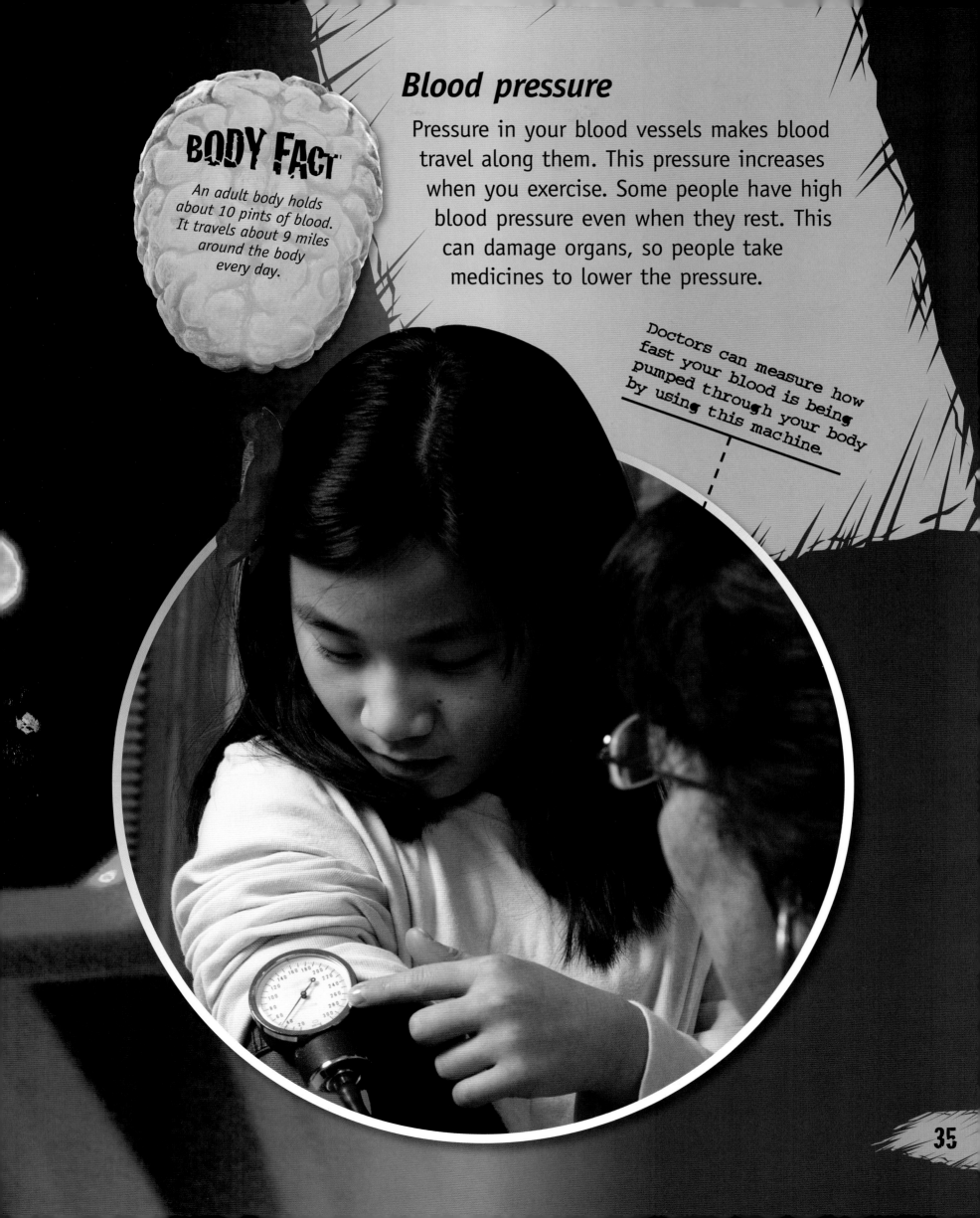

Blood pressure

Pressure in your blood vessels makes blood travel along them. This pressure increases when you exercise. Some people have high blood pressure even when they rest. This can damage organs, so people take medicines to lower the pressure.

BODY FACT

An adult body holds about 10 pints of blood. It travels about 9 miles around the body every day.

Doctors can measure how fast your blood is being pumped through your body by using this machine.

YOUR BEATING HEART

Your heart is a muscle about the size of your fist. It beats around 60–90 times every minute, pumping blood to every part of your body.

Blood in from the body

Four chambers

Your heart has four chambers. The two chambers on the right side are separated from the two chambers on the left side by a thick wall of muscle. The top chambers on each side fill up with blood from large blood vessels. The blood then passes into the two chambers below. From there it is pumped out through large blood vessels.

The two sides of the heart work together to pump the blood.

You can feel your heartbeat if you place your hand on your chest over your heart.

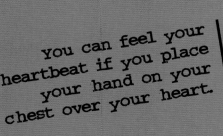

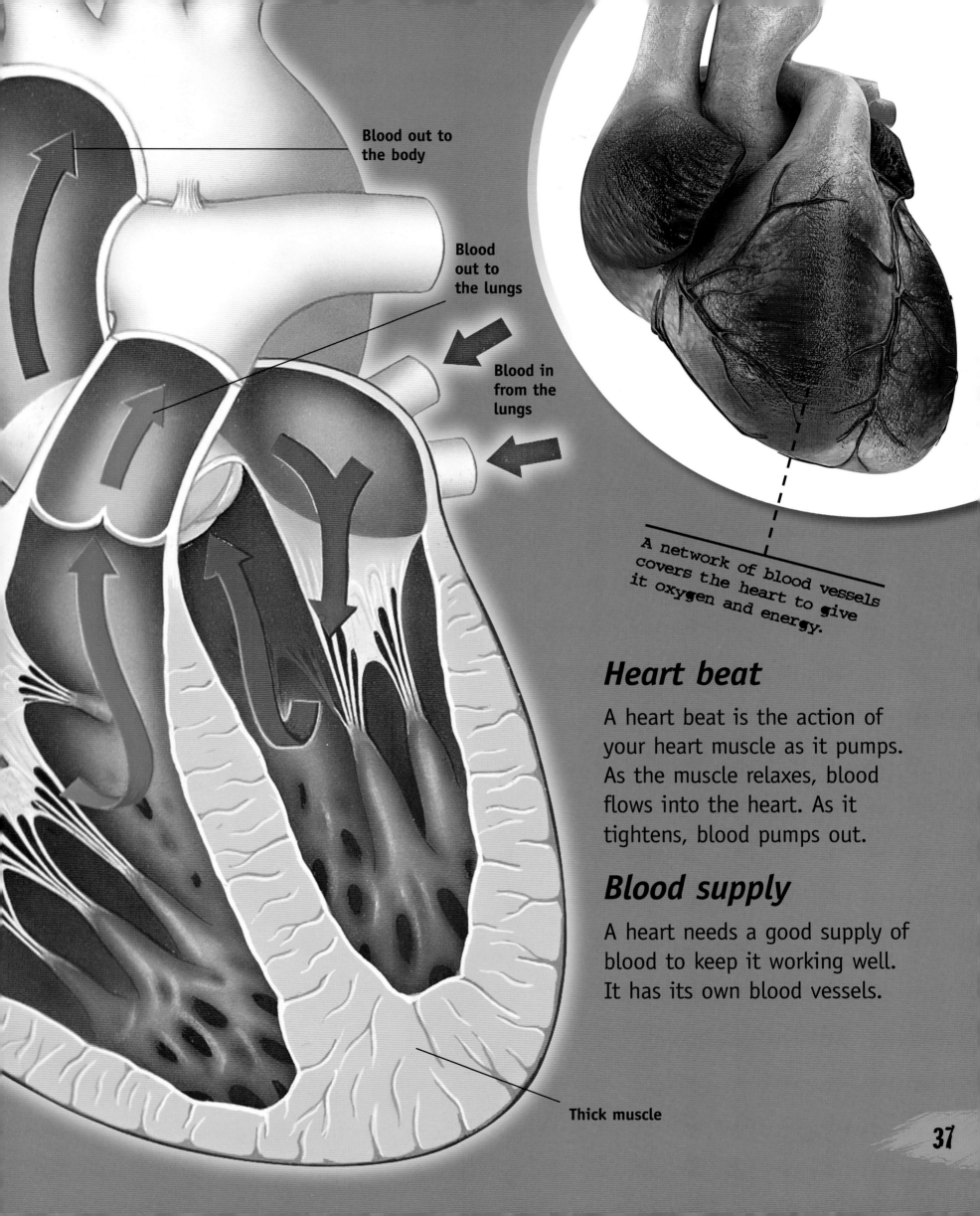

Blood out to the body

Blood out to the lungs

Blood in from the lungs

A network of blood vessels covers the heart to give it oxygen and energy.

Thick muscle

Heart beat

A heart beat is the action of your heart muscle as it pumps. As the muscle relaxes, blood flows into the heart. As it tightens, blood pumps out.

Blood supply

A heart needs a good supply of blood to keep it working well. It has its own blood vessels.

A HEALTHY HEART

Your heart works hard all your life. It's important to keep it in good condition.

Working harder

Your heart has to work harder when you exercise to pump more blood to your muscles. To do this, it beats faster—up to 200 times a minute. It also beats faster if you are anxious—for example, if you are watching a scary movie.

BODY FACT

Doctors can replace some parts of the heart if they stop working correctly.

Exercise, such as running, makes your heart work faster. This keeps it healthy.

Healthy heart

It is important to keep your heart healthy. You can do so by doing a lot of exercise to keep the heart muscle strong. What you eat also affects the health of your heart. Do not eat too much animal fat. This is found in red meat, cream, butter, and cheese. Smoking cigarettes and drinking alcohol can also damage your heart.

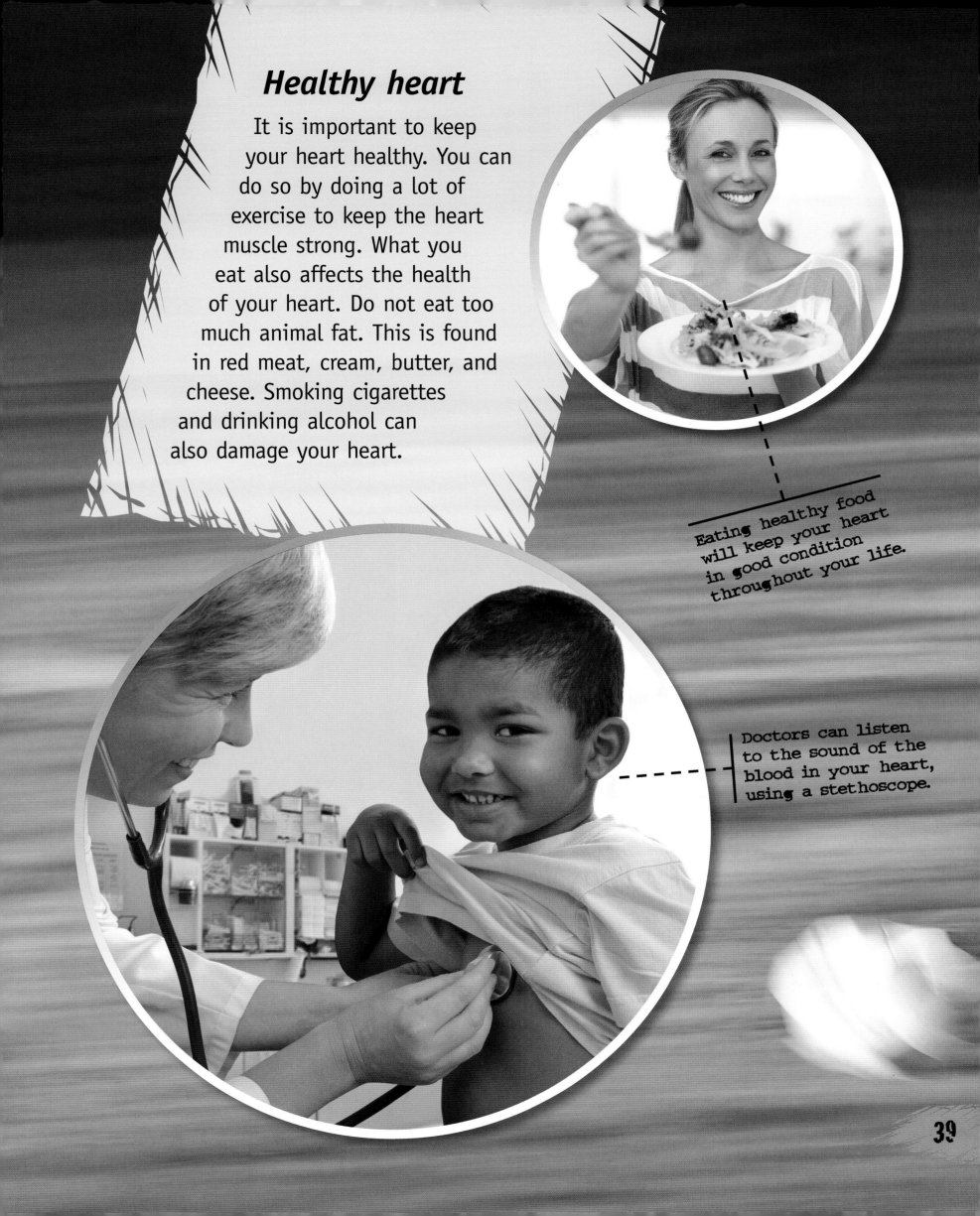

Eating healthy food will keep your heart in good condition throughout your life.

Doctors can listen to the sound of the blood in your heart, using a stethoscope.

BRILLIANT BLOOD

Blood is the sticky red liquid that comes out through your skin when you cut yourself. It is part of the transportation system that carries substances around your body.

What is in blood?

Blood is made of a mixture of a watery liquid called **plasma**, and blood cells. It contains **red blood cells** and **white blood cells**. There are many more red blood cells than white ones.

Blood is red and white blood cells in plasma.

Blood vessel

Plasma

White blood cell

Red blood cell

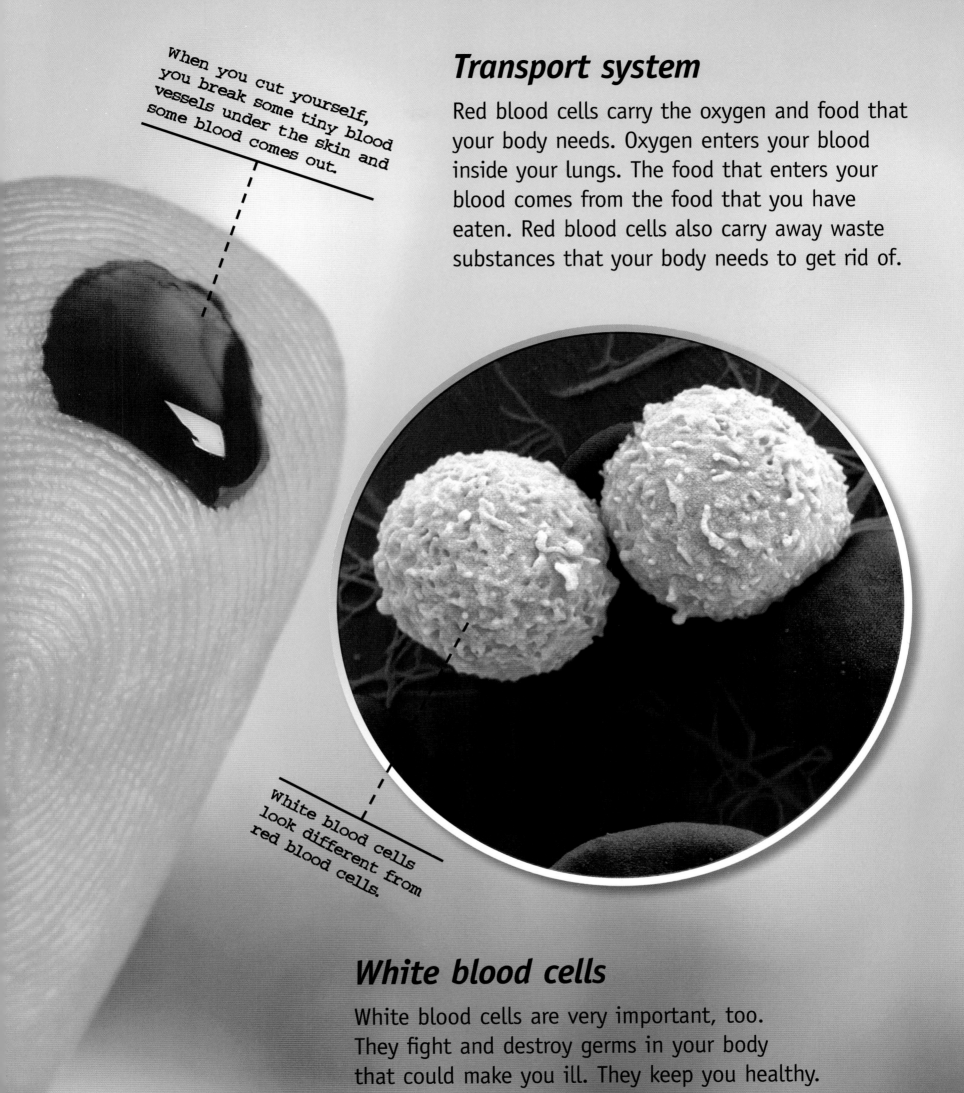

When you cut yourself, you break some tiny blood vessels under the skin and some blood comes out.

Transport system

Red blood cells carry the oxygen and food that your body needs. Oxygen enters your blood inside your lungs. The food that enters your blood comes from the food that you have eaten. Red blood cells also carry away waste substances that your body needs to get rid of.

White blood cells look different from red blood cells.

White blood cells

White blood cells are very important, too. They fight and destroy germs in your body that could make you ill. They keep you healthy.

BLEEDING AND MENDING

Your clever blood helps repair any damage caused when you hurt yourself.

Why is blood red?

Blood is red because of all the red blood cells in it. Red blood cells get their color from a substance in them called **hemoglobin**. This substance carries the oxygen in the blood cells.

BODY FACT

There are different kinds of white blood cells. They do different jobs to protect you from germs.

A red blood cell is round and flat, with a dip in the middle.

Mending damage

When you cut yourself, your blood repairs the damage and stops germs from getting into it. Blood cells clump together to stop the bleeding and make a patch over the cut. This is a scab. White blood cells kill any germs that have entered the body. New skin then starts to grow under the scab.

Bruises

If you knock your skin hard but do not cut it, you may get a bruise. A bruise appears if you break the small blood vessels under your skin. Some blood leaks out into your skin and shows as red or purple.

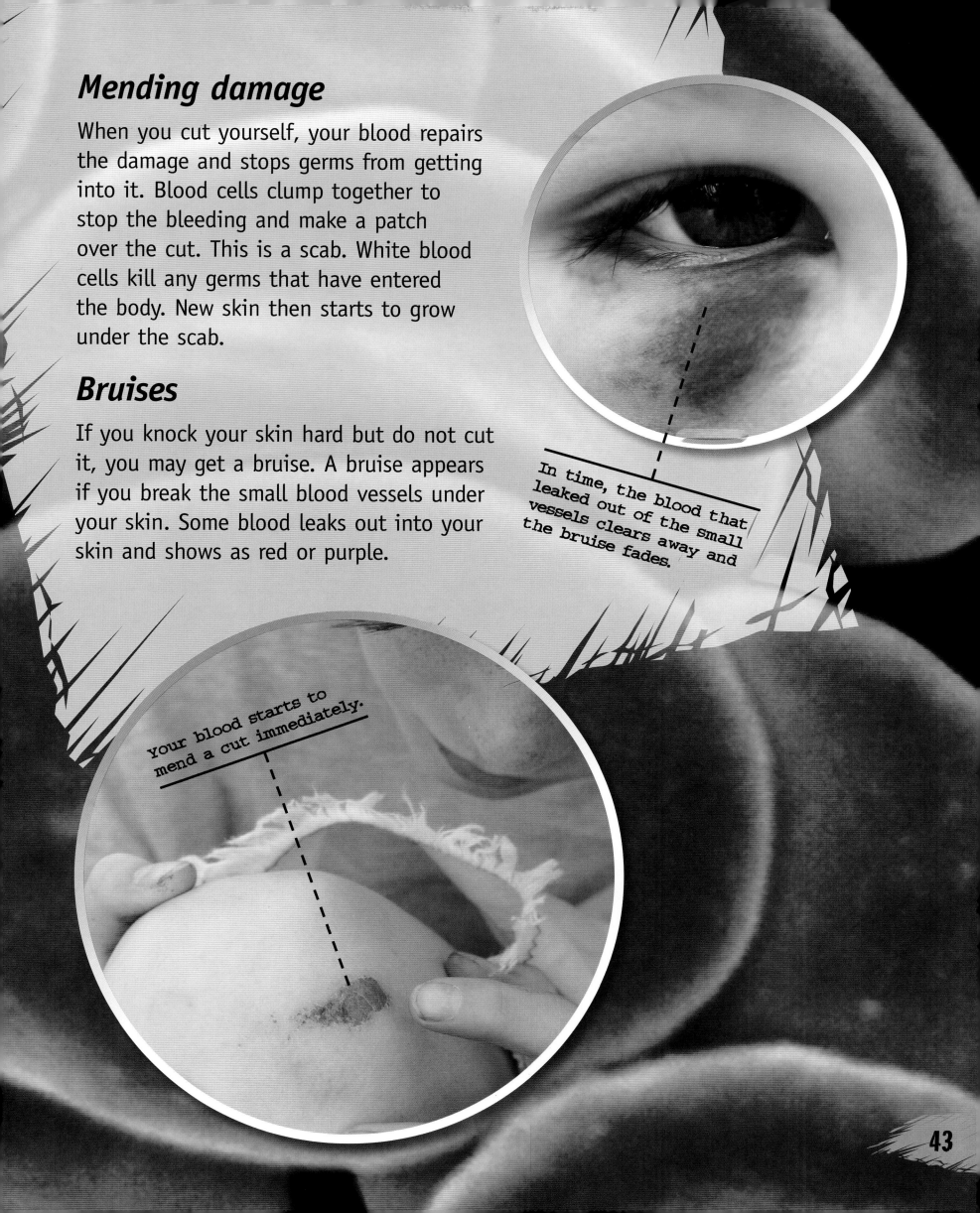

In time, the blood that leaked out of the small vessels clears away and the bruise fades.

Your blood starts to mend a cut immediately.

43

PROTECTING FROM GERMS

Germs are everywhere. Many of them do not harm you, but some can make you unwell. Your body has many ways of protecting you from them.

What are germs?

Germs are too small to see, but they are all around you. There are two kinds of germs: **bacteria** and **viruses**. If these get inside you, they can make you ill. Bacteria cause illnesses such as food poisoning. Viruses cause illnesses such as colds.

This picture shows bacteria on a kitchen scouring pad.

BODY FACT

The oil that your skin produces to make it waterproof can destroy some germs.

Droplets in a sneeze can travel 32 feet and other people can breathe them in.

Spreading germs

You spread germs by touching things. You carry the germs on your skin to a new surface. You also spread germs when you cough or sneeze. If you do not cover your mouth, germs shoot out into the air in tiny droplets.

Helpful body

Your body helps protect you from germs in lots of ways. Your main defence is your skin. It stops germs from getting into your body and makes sweat that washes germs away.

Germs on your hands are spread when you touch things.

45

INSIDE AND OUT

Some parts of your body protect you from germs outside you. Others work on the germs that get inside your body.

Eyes and ears

Your eyes produce tears that wash away germs. Your nose helps, too. It makes a thick sticky liquid that traps germs that get up your nose. Blowing your nose gets rid of them.

Blowing your nose gets rid of germs.

BODY FACT

You can kill the germs in food by washing it before you eat it and by cooking it at high temperatures.

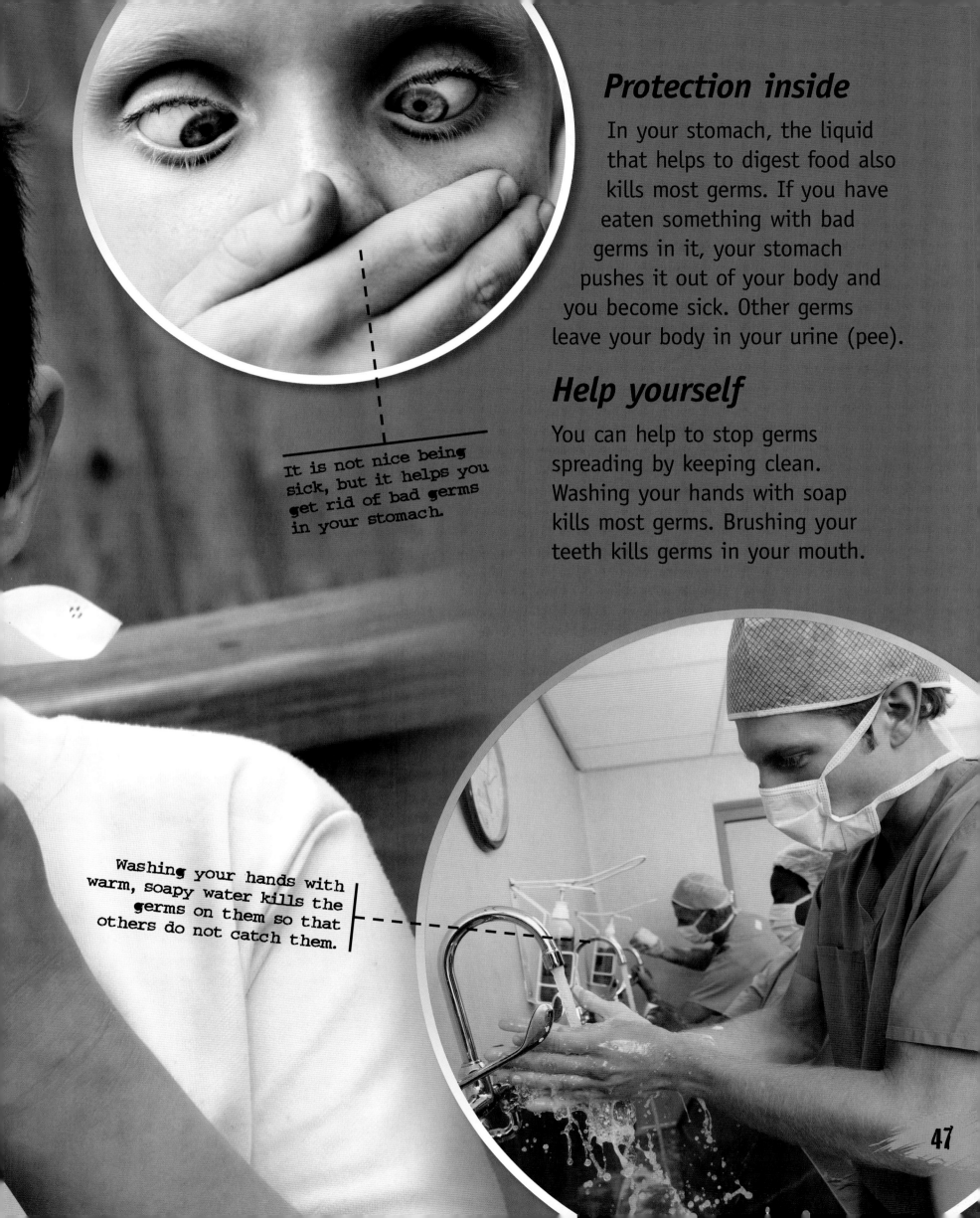

Protection inside

In your stomach, the liquid that helps to digest food also kills most germs. If you have eaten something with bad germs in it, your stomach pushes it out of your body and you become sick. Other germs leave your body in your urine (pee).

It is not nice being sick, but it helps you get rid of bad germs in your stomach.

Help yourself

You can help to stop germs spreading by keeping clean. Washing your hands with soap kills most germs. Brushing your teeth kills germs in your mouth.

Washing your hands with warm, soapy water kills the germs on them so that others do not catch them.

47

FIGHTING INFECTION

If germs get inside your body, they can cause an **infection**. However, your body has a brilliant system for fighting infections and making you better.

Immune system

Germs get into your body through cuts in your skin or through openings such as those of your nose. Then white blood cells in your blood start attacking them. They swallow the germs, then carry them off to your liver and kidneys. Here more white blood cells destroy them.

Here, a white blood cell (red) is surrounding and destroying a germ (green).

48

Fever

If you have a bad infection, your white blood cells produce a substance that makes you hotter and raises your temperature. You must rest while your body fights the infection.

Protection

Doctors can protect you from some serious infections. They may give you an injection of some germs that will not harm you. Your body then learns how to fight them so that you are not bothered by those same germs in future.

Children all over the world are given injections to protect them from serious infections.

BREATHING TO LIVE

You must breathe air to live. When you breathe in, air enters your lungs. When you breathe out, you push air out again.

Breath for life

Air contains oxygen, which your body needs. When you breathe in, air passes down a pipe into a system of tubes. Inside your lungs, these tubes become smaller and smaller. They end in tiny air sacs. This network of tubes is a lung. You have two lungs.

Right lung

Lungs are made of branching air tubes that end in air sacs and branching blood vessels.

Air sacs

Tiny blood vessels cover the air sacs.

Blood vessels

Branching air tubes

Blood vessels

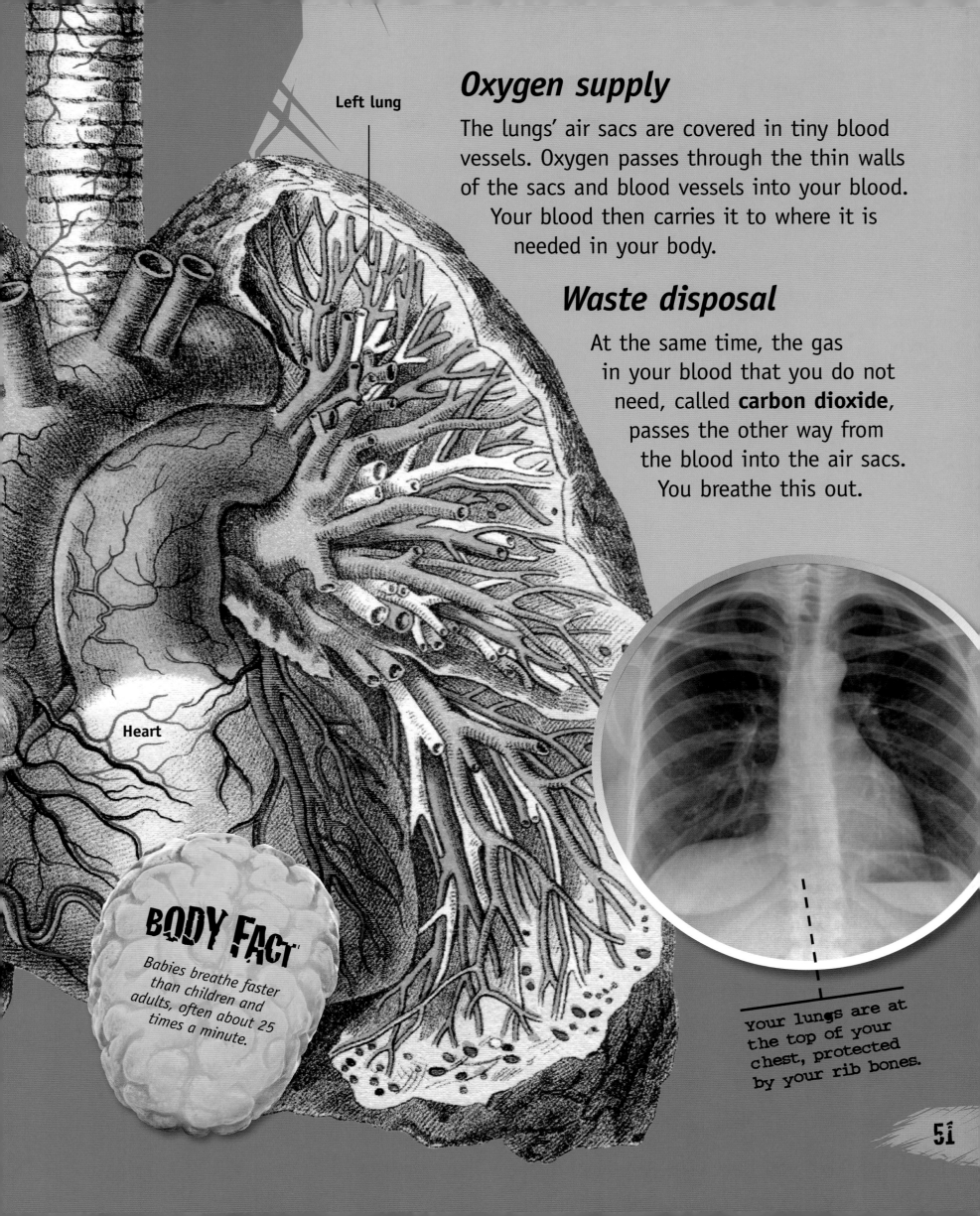

Left lung

Oxygen supply

The lungs' air sacs are covered in tiny blood vessels. Oxygen passes through the thin walls of the sacs and blood vessels into your blood. Your blood then carries it to where it is needed in your body.

Waste disposal

At the same time, the gas in your blood that you do not need, called **carbon dioxide**, passes the other way from the blood into the air sacs. You breathe this out.

Heart

BODY FACT

Babies breathe faster than children and adults, often about 25 times a minute.

Your lungs are at the top of your chest, protected by your rib bones.

IN, OUT

All day and all night, you continue to breathe in and out.

Breathing in and out

Your lungs are protected by your ribs, and below them is a muscle called the **diaphragm**. When you breathe in, the diaphragm tightens and moves down, and the ribs move out. This makes room for your lungs to fill with air. As you breathe out, your diaphragm relaxes, the ribs move back in, and air is pushed out of your lungs.

Your chest gets bigger when you breathe in.

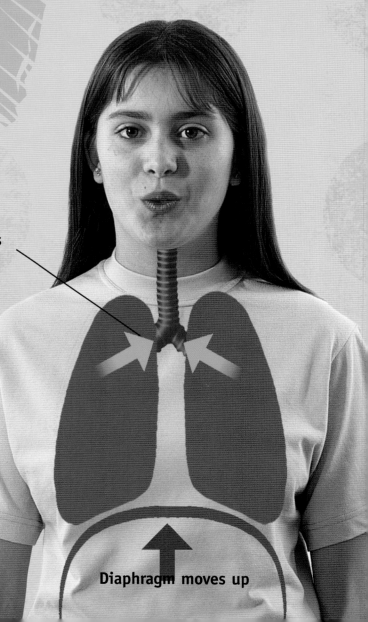

Air into lungs

Air out of lungs

Diaphragm moves down

Diaphragm moves up

Breathing fast and slow

When you are resting, you breathe slowly and gently. When you exercise, your body needs more oxygen, so you take more breaths. You breathe more deeply, too.

When you stop exercising, you may keep panting to take in more oxygen.

Asthma

People have asthma when their air tubes become narrow and sticky with mucus. This makes breathing difficult. Asthma sufferers can breathe in a medicine through an inhaler, to open the air tubes and make them less sticky.

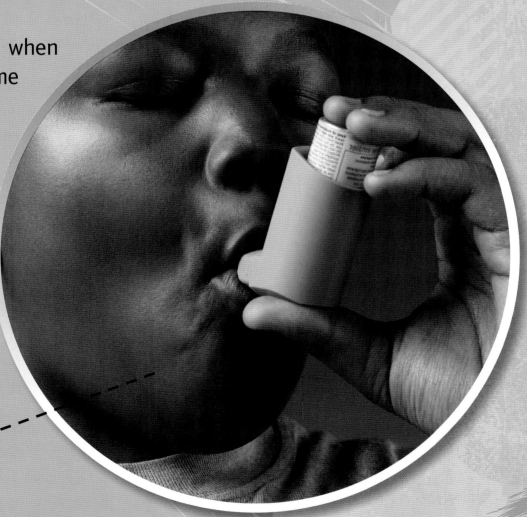

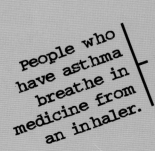

People who have asthma breathe in medicine from an inhaler.

FOOD FOR FUEL

Your body needs food to keep working. Food gives you energy and makes you grow bigger too.

Regular meals

Your body needs food regularly, to give you energy. You usually eat several meals a day to keep your energy supply topped up. The food we eat comes in many different forms. We eat some things raw and other things we cook first.

The group of organs that works to turn the food you eat into energy for your body is called your digestive system.

Tongue

Stomach

Large intestine

Small intestine

In it goes

Food goes into your body through your mouth. You chew it with your teeth to break it into smaller pieces. Your tongue helps to move it around. Then you swallow it and it goes into a long tube. It takes only a few seconds to then reach your stomach.

A meal can be a social occasion where we talk to each other while we eat.

BODY FACT

Eating 12 French fries gives you the same amount of energy as seven carrots or 33 sticks of celery.

Saliva

The spit in your mouth is called **saliva**. It contains substances that start to break down food.

Your mouth produces saliva when you start to eat.

A HEALTHY DIET

The kinds of foods you put into your body affect how well it works. It is important to eat the right kinds of foods to stay healthy.

What kinds of foods?

Each type of food contains different substances that your body needs. Bread, pasta, and rice give you **carbohydrates**. They are good for energy. Vegetables and fruit contain **vitamins** and **minerals** to help your organs work. Meat, fish, eggs, and cheese give you **protein** to help your body grow and make repairs.

Fatty and sugary foods should be a treat you have sometimes, not a big part of your diet.

BODY FACT

During your lifetime, you will drink about 105,000 pints of liquid.

Make sure your meals contain a mixture of the different food types, and do not eat too much.

Delicious dishes

Foods can be combined and cooked to make a huge variety of dishes and flavors.

Drinking

Your body needs lots of liquid, so drink plenty of water every day. On hot days, you should drink even more to replace the liquid your body loses as sweat.

There are so many delicious foods to try.

DIGESTING YOUR FOOD

Your body works hard to take what it needs from food. This process is called **digestion**.

Breaking food down

In your stomach, muscles churn up food with liquids that help break it down. The good things in your food are called **nutrients**. Different nutrients are taken in by your body at different stages of digestion. From the stomach, the mixture goes into the **small intestine**.

BODY FACT

A meal takes one or two days to travel from one end of your digestive system to the other.

This picture of an intestine was taken by a tiny camera that was placed inside the body.

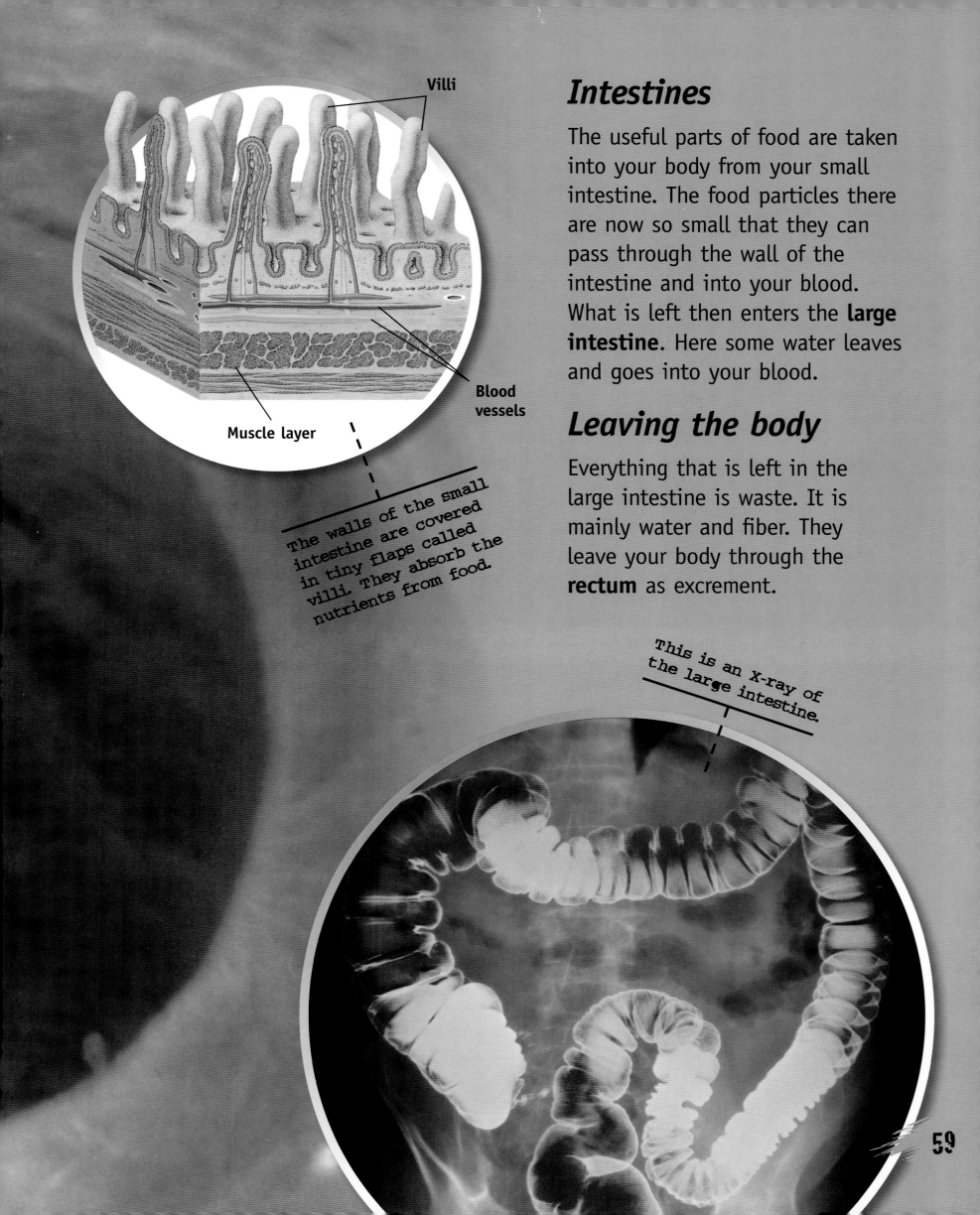

Villi

Muscle layer

Blood vessels

The walls of the small intestine are covered in tiny flaps called villi. They absorb the nutrients from food.

Intestines

The useful parts of food are taken into your body from your small intestine. The food particles there are now so small that they can pass through the wall of the intestine and into your blood. What is left then enters the **large intestine**. Here some water leaves and goes into your blood.

Leaving the body

Everything that is left in the large intestine is waste. It is mainly water and fiber. They leave your body through the **rectum** as excrement.

This is an X-ray of the large intestine.

PROCESSING WASTE

Some waste products are removed from your body by your kidneys, which clean your blood. The waste then leaves your body in your urine.

Clever kidneys

Waste substances in your body collect in your large intestine and in your blood. They must be removed. The waste in your intestine leaves the body as excrement. Your kidneys clean the waste from your blood by turning it into urine.

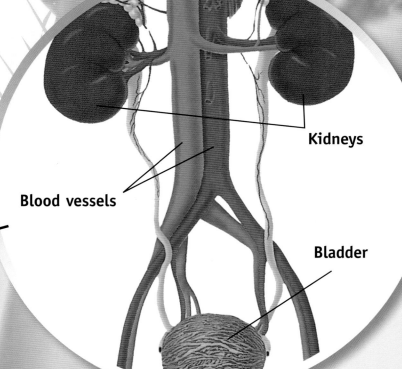

You feel thirsty when your brain says your body needs more water.

Kidneys

Blood vessels

Bladder

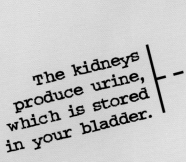

The kidneys produce urine, which is stored in your bladder.

When your urine is pale, you are drinking enough water. If it is dark, you should drink more.

Time to go

Your brain tells you when your bladder is full and you need to use the bathroom. It also tells you when you are thirsty and need to drink.

BODY FACT

All the blood in your body passes through your kidneys every ten minutes, so your blood is cleaned about 150 times every day.

AN AMAZING BRAIN

Your brain is the control center for your body. It tells every part of you what to do, using your nerves as messengers.

What is your brain for?

You use your brain to think, to make all your senses work, to move, to talk, to remember, and just to stay alive. It is much more powerful than any computer, and it can do many different things at once. For example, you can think while you look and listen, or speak while you walk.

An adult brain weighs about 11 pounds.

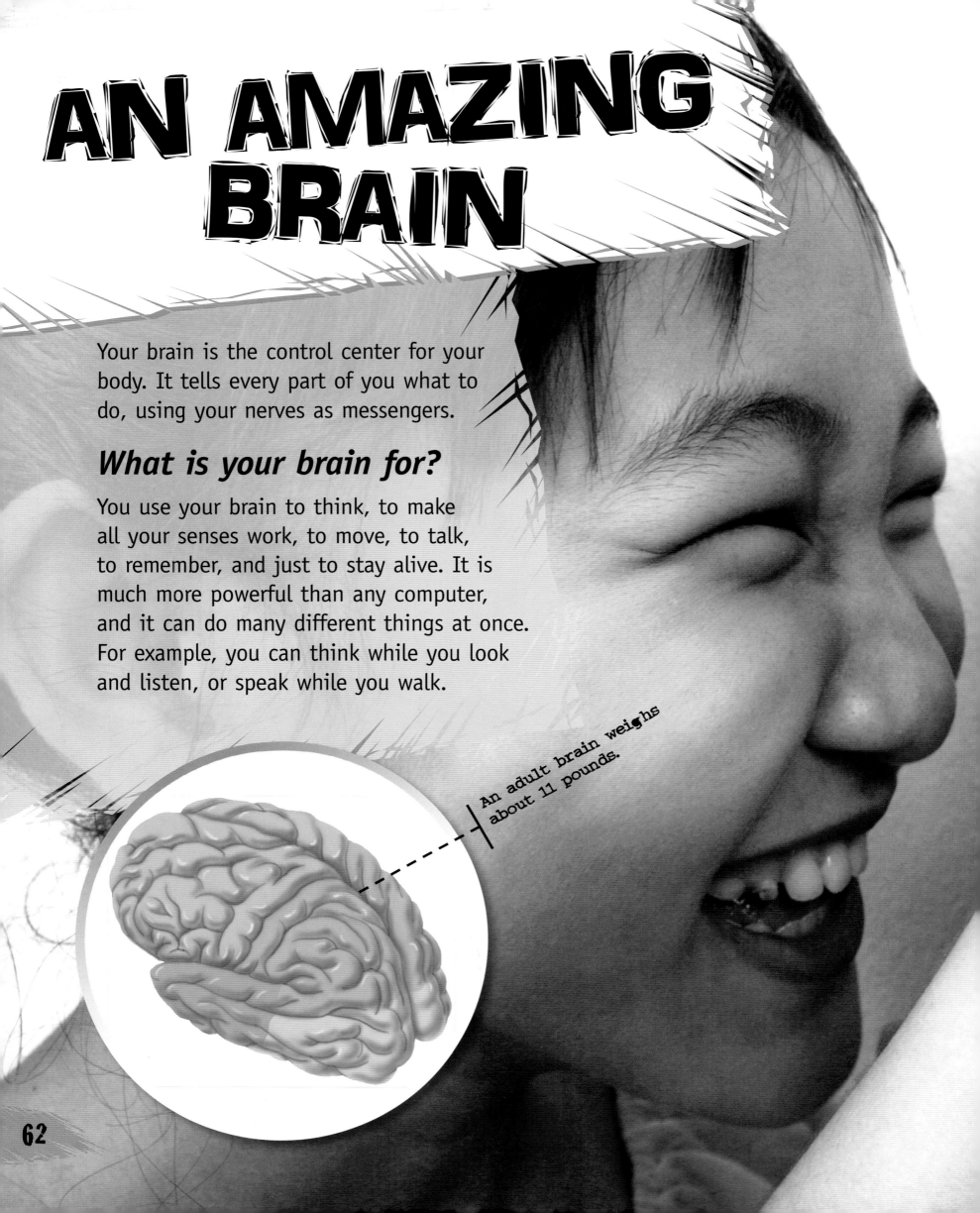

What does your brain look like?

Your brain is about the size of your two fists put together. It has two halves. These are joined together in the middle of the brain. The surface of the brain is gray and wrinkled. Your skull bone protects the brain inside your head.

Everything you do is controlled by your brain.

BODY FACT

Men have slightly bigger brains than women, but there is no link between the size of your brain and how clever you are.

INSIDE YOUR BRAIN

Your brain is very complicated. Scientists are working hard to understand how it can do so many different jobs at once.

What is inside your brain?

Different parts of your brain have different jobs to do. Each of your senses is controlled by a separate part of the brain. Thinking and feeling are controlled by an area at the front. Balance and movement are controlled at the back. Your heart and lungs are controlled by an area deep inside the middle.

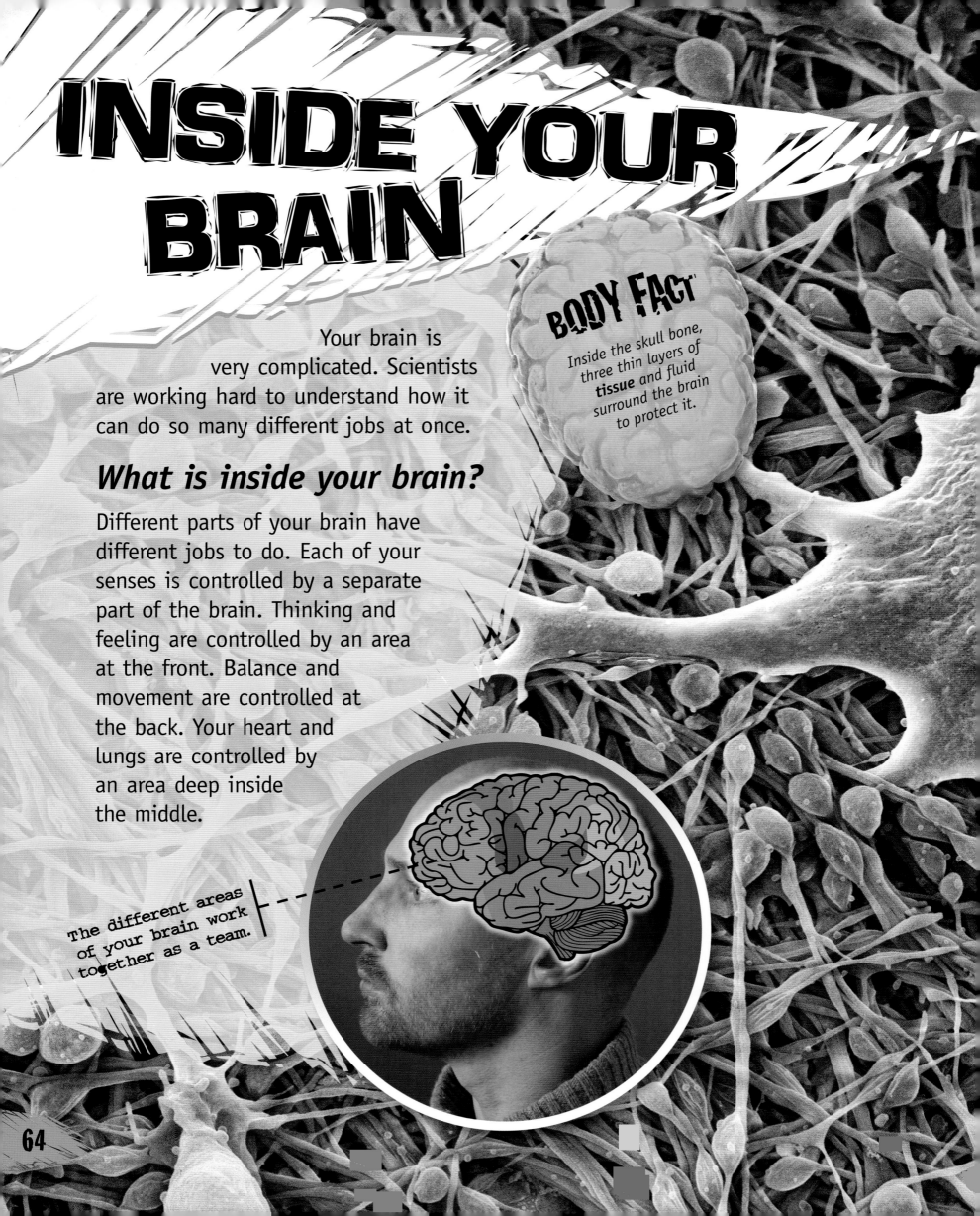

The different areas of your brain work together as a team.

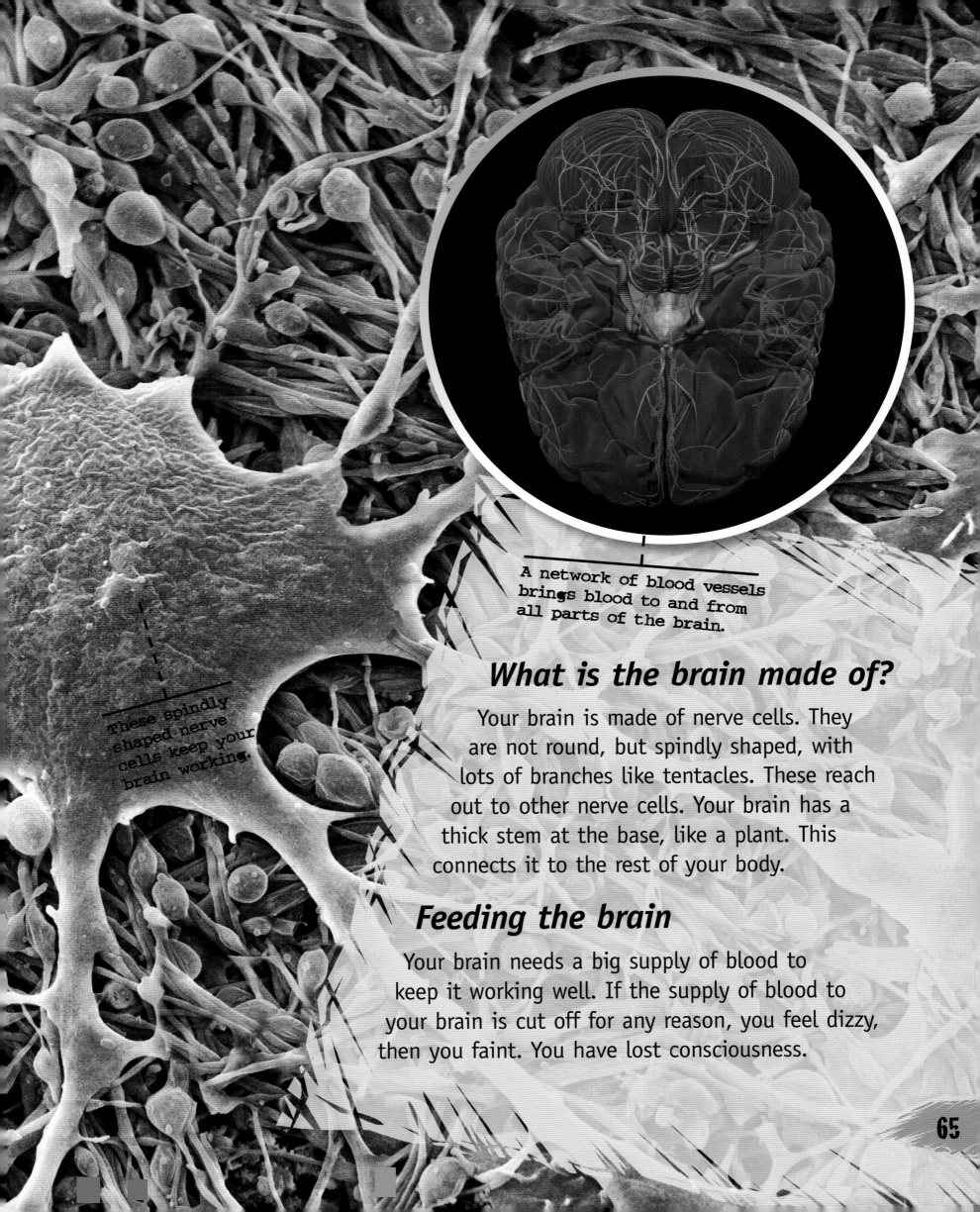

A network of blood vessels brings blood to and from all parts of the brain.

These spindly shaped nerve cells keep your brain working.

What is the brain made of?

Your brain is made of nerve cells. They are not round, but spindly shaped, with lots of branches like tentacles. These reach out to other nerve cells. Your brain has a thick stem at the base, like a plant. This connects it to the rest of your body.

Feeding the brain

Your brain needs a big supply of blood to keep it working well. If the supply of blood to your brain is cut off for any reason, you feel dizzy, then you faint. You have lost consciousness.

YOUR NERVOUS SYSTEM

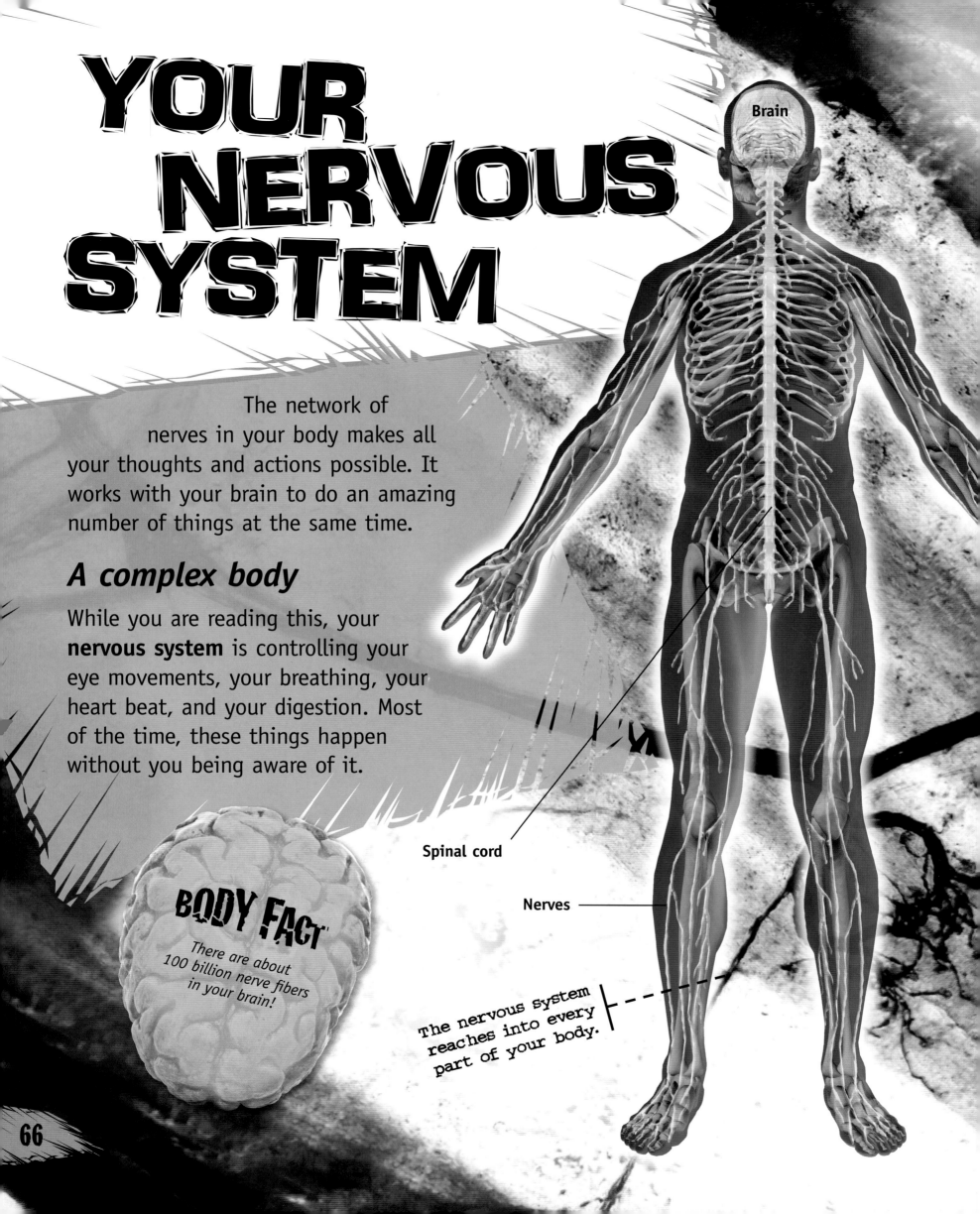

Brain

The network of nerves in your body makes all your thoughts and actions possible. It works with your brain to do an amazing number of things at the same time.

A complex body

While you are reading this, your **nervous system** is controlling your eye movements, your breathing, your heart beat, and your digestion. Most of the time, these things happen without you being aware of it.

BODY FACT

There are about 100 billion nerve fibers in your brain!

Spinal cord

Nerves

The nervous system reaches into every part of your body.

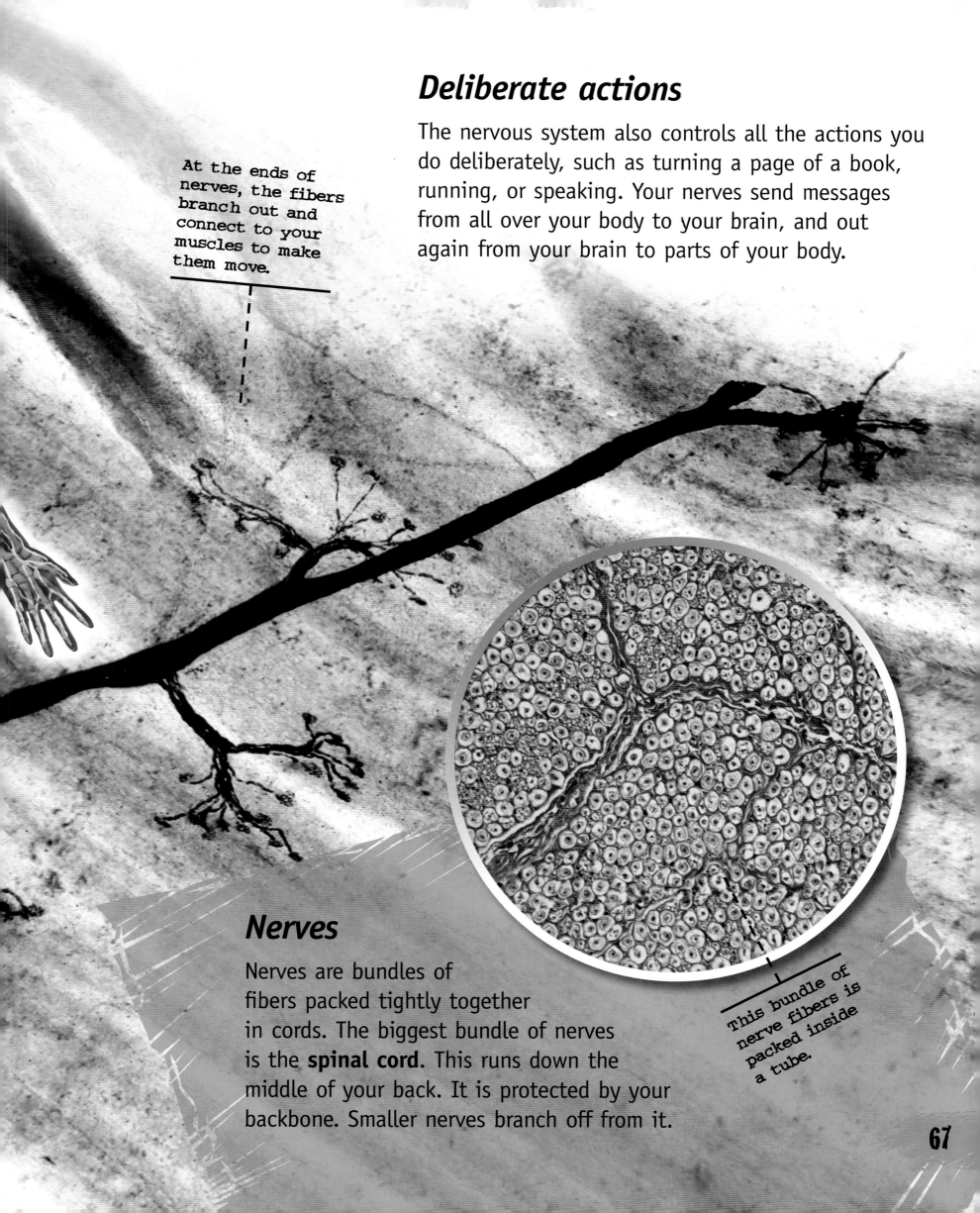

Deliberate actions

The nervous system also controls all the actions you do deliberately, such as turning a page of a book, running, or speaking. Your nerves send messages from all over your body to your brain, and out again from your brain to parts of your body.

At the ends of nerves, the fibers branch out and connect to your muscles to make them move.

Nerves

Nerves are bundles of fibers packed tightly together in cords. The biggest bundle of nerves is the **spinal cord**. This runs down the middle of your back. It is protected by your backbone. Smaller nerves branch off from it.

This bundle of nerve fibers is packed inside a tube.

SENDING MESSAGES

Your nerves are the body's messengers. They carry their messages so amazingly fast that you don't even notice them doing it.

Speedy messages

The starter says "Go!" and the race begins. A message from your ears tells your brain about the sound from the voice. Your brain knows what 'Go!' means. It sends messages along your nerves to your muscles. It tells them to move, to make you run. You start to move as fast as you can. All of this takes less than one second!

BODY FACT

Messages travel along the nervous system at speeds of up to 180 miles an hour!

If only we could run as fast as the messages that travel along our nervous system!

Confusing the brain

Your brain tries to make sense of what your eyes, ears, and other senses tell it. Sometimes it is not sure how to do this. A picture that confuses your brain about what it means is called an **optical illusion**.

Your brain cannot tell if this picture shows two heads facing each other, or a white vase on a black background. It is an optical illusion.

STAYING ALIVE

Some things happen in your body without you thinking about them. You need them to happen to stay alive.

Day and night

Every minute of your life, your heart is beating and you are breathing. You do not have to tell your heart and lungs to do this. Also, your digestive system keeps working on the food you have eaten. All these actions are controlled by part of your nervous system. From deep in your brain, nerves send out messages to these parts of your body.

Everyone feels nervous sometimes.

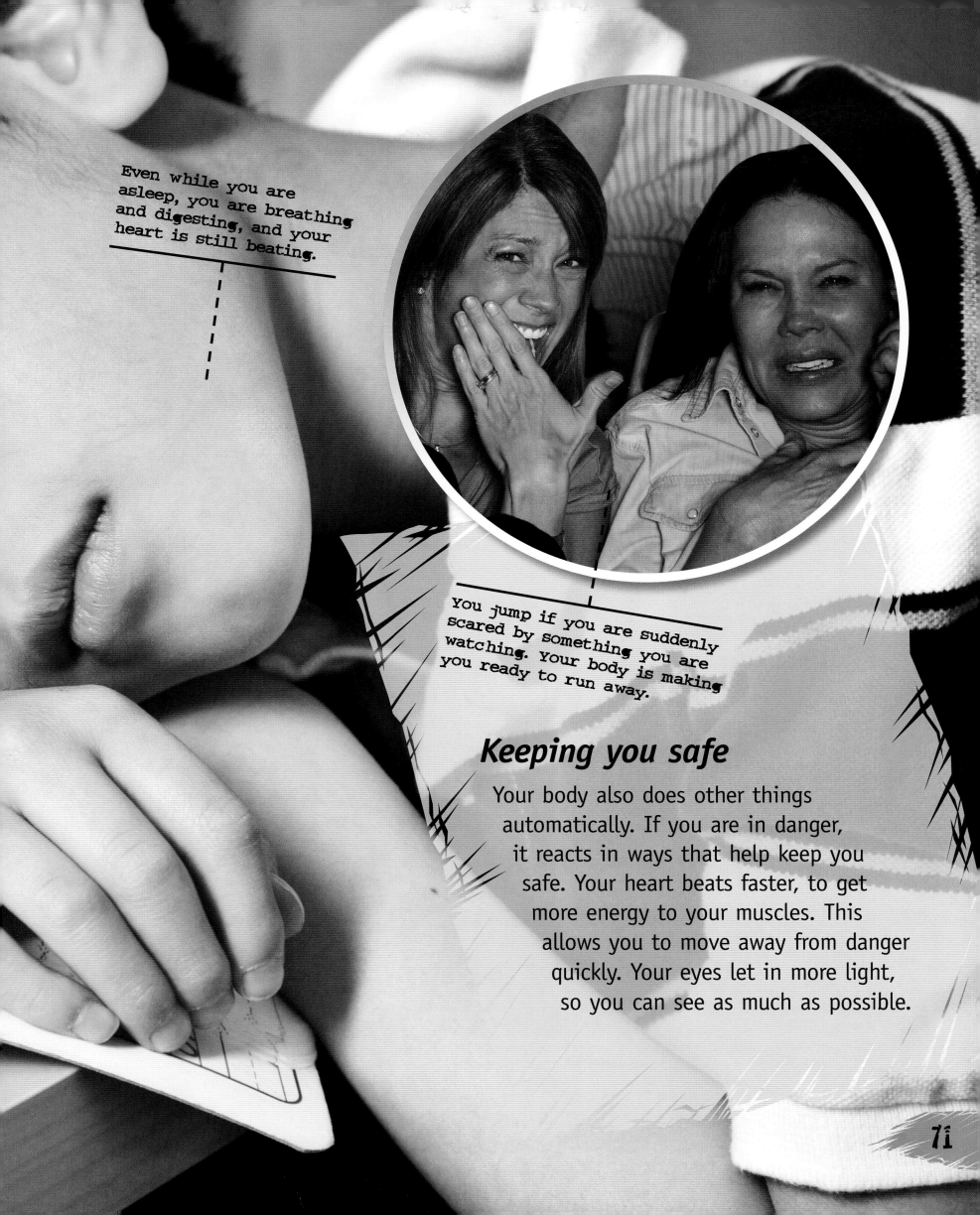

Even while you are asleep, you are breathing and digesting, and your heart is still beating.

You jump if you are suddenly scared by something you are watching. Your body is making you ready to run away.

Keeping you safe

Your body also does other things automatically. If you are in danger, it reacts in ways that help keep you safe. Your heart beats faster, to get more energy to your muscles. This allows you to move away from danger quickly. Your eyes let in more light, so you can see as much as possible.

LEARNING AND MEMORY

Every day you are learning new things. You learn by remembering things you are told or that have happened to you.

How do you learn?

You use an area at the top part of your brain to learn. You have an amazing ability to store information in your brain. You can also recall that information when you need it to remember something. But you cannot remember every tiny thing that happens. Your brain selects things to store as memories.

young children learn by exploring everything they can get their hands on.

When you read, you use your memory to recollect letters and words.

Asking questions

You learn by asking questions about the world around you. If you touch a stinging nettle and it hurts, you learn not to touch nettles again. If you find a food you like, you learn to ask for it again.

The part of your brain that is used for memory is shown in pink on this scan of a brain.

Helpful teaching

Sometimes it is helpful if other people teach us a new skill. You learned to read with the help of an adult. Your brain listened to what they told you and stored it in your memory. The next time you tried reading, you remembered it.

MEMORIES FOR LIFE

Your brain builds up a store of memories throughout your life. Some things you remember for a few days. Other memories stay with you for ever.

How long do you remember?

Your brain stores some memories for a short time and other memories for longer. Short-term memories are things like what you ate for lunch yesterday. Long-term memories are things like your first day at school, or a great holiday. You can store millions of these, and remember them for many years ahead.

People can get to know each other better by listening to their memories.

Valuable memories

Memories can bring people together when they share them. It can be wonderful to hear about the past from older people. They remember interesting things that happened before you were born. You can tell them your memories, too.

Card games test your short-term memory.

BODY FACT

Your short-term memory becomes weaker as you grow older, but your long-term memory often stays strong.

You are never too old to learn a new skill. It keeps your brain active.

Use it or lose it

Learning does not end after school. All your life you can keep your brain healthy by learning new things and having new experiences. There is always more to learn and more fun to have!

75

YOUR SENSE OF TOUCH

You feel things through your skin. Nerve endings in your skin send messages to your brain.

How you feel

As you are reading this, what can you feel? Perhaps the pages of the book, the chair you are sitting on, and the temperature of the air around you. Your sense of touch is telling you all these things.

BODY FACT

The nerves in your skin are called touch receptors. There are thousands of touch receptors in one fingertip.

The two oval shapes are nerve endings in your skin. The red area is the top layer of your skin.

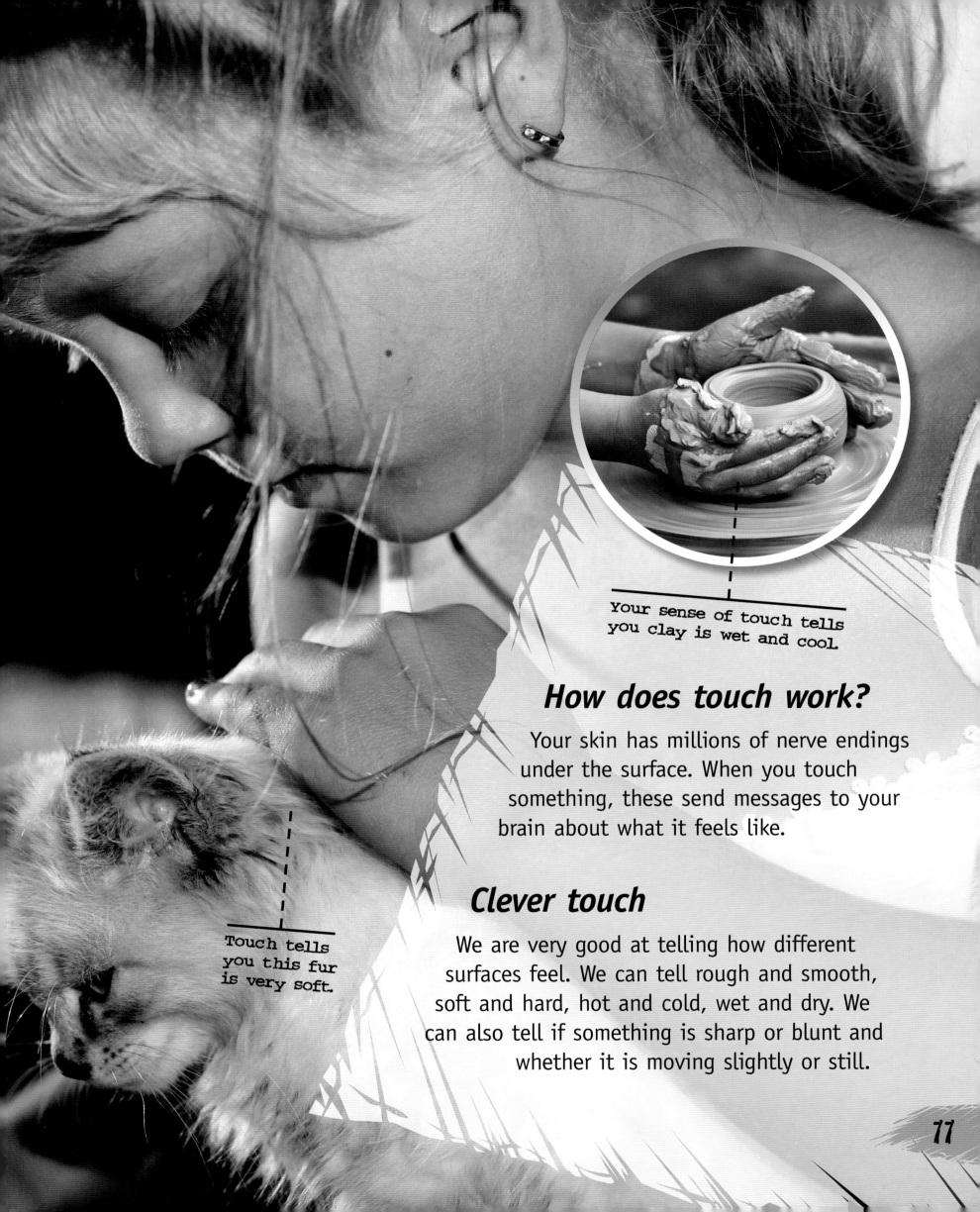

Your sense of touch tells you clay is wet and cool

Touch tells you this fur is very soft.

How does touch work?

Your skin has millions of nerve endings under the surface. When you touch something, these send messages to your brain about what it feels like.

Clever touch

We are very good at telling how different surfaces feel. We can tell rough and smooth, soft and hard, hot and cold, wet and dry. We can also tell if something is sharp or blunt and whether it is moving slightly or still.

TOUCHING AND FEELING

Your sense of touch helps you to avoid danger and to learn about the world around you.

Sensitive skin

Some parts of the skin are more sensitive than others. The tips of your fingers are especially good at feeling things. So are your lips and your tongue. The rest of your skin is less sensitive. Places where the skin is thick, such as the soles of your feet, are less good at detecting touch.

BODY FACT
When you feel something you usually look at it as well. If you feel something you cannot see, it is difficult to work out what it is.

Some parts of the skin can feel the lightest touch.

Feeling pain

When you hurt yourself on something, you quickly pull away from it. The pain signal is sent along the nerves to your spine and your muscles react by pulling you away. The pain signal also goes to your brain, which tells you it hurts!

You react quickly when you feel pain.

Reading by touch

Using touch, people who cannot see can read by feeling a pattern of raised dots. Each pattern represents a letter of the alphabet. This system is called **Braille**.

Braille is named after the French man who invented it: Louis Braille.

79

YOUR SENSE OF SIGHT

You see with your eyes. They take in thousands of images every day, which are sent to your brain.

How do eyes work?

Your eyes let in light through the black dot in the middle, called the **pupil**. Behind the pupil, there is a **lens**. This makes a picture of what you are looking at, on a place at the back of your eye called the **retina**. The retina sends messages about what you see to your brain.

Pupil

Lens

Retina

Using both your eyes together helps you tell how far away an object is.

Light or dark

In a dark place, the pupil opens more to let in more light to help you see. In a bright light, the pupil closes up. Too much light can harm your eye.

Seeing colors

You can see colors because there are special cells in your retina that detect them.

Your eyes can tell the difference between hundreds of different colors.

The pupil controls how much light enters your eye.

PRECIOUS EYES

Everyone's eyes look slightly different, but they all work in the same way and they all need to be looked after.

Eye color

The colored part of your eye is called the **iris**. As well as color, it also has a pattern. Everyone has a different color and pattern. The color is affected by how much melanin is in your pupil. This is the exact same substance that decides the color of your hair and the color of skin.

Darker eyes have more melanin in the iris.

82

Glasses correct faults in your eyes so that you can see clearly.

Always shade your eyes from bright sunlight.

Correcting problems

Sometimes people's eyes do not work properly. They cannot see a clear image of what they are looking at. Some people cannot see things clearly that are far away. Other people cannot see things that are close up. This can happen at any age. You can wear glasses over your eyes to correct this problem.

Protecting your eyes

Bright light from the Sun can damage your eyes. You should protect them by wearing dark glasses, or by shading your eyes with a hat. Never look at the Sun, even with dark glasses on. You could go blind.

YOUR SENSE OF HEARING

You hear with your ears. A sound is a vibration in the air, like a ripple on a pond. Your ears take in these sounds and make them louder.

How do ears work?

Sound vibrations in the air enter your ears. Inside your head, they reach the **eardrum**. This is a thin surface, as a drum has. Vibrations pass through it. Then they reach some very small bones, which move when they are hit by the sound. Nerves pick up these movements and send messages about what you are hearing to your brain.

There is more of your ear inside your head than outside.

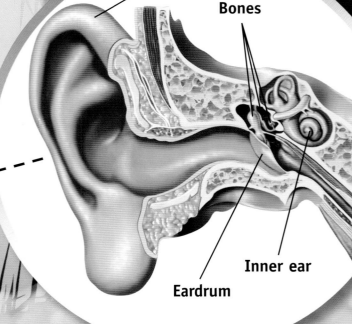

Ear

Bones

Inner ear

Eardrum

Your ears can pick out lots of different sounds in a noisy place.

Sound direction

You have two ears that help you tell which direction sounds are coming from. Sounds reach one ear before the other.

Measuring sound

Sound is measured in units called **decibels**. Normal talking is about 60 decibels. A loud music concert is about 100 decibels. Anything louder than 85 decibels can damage your ears. So keep the volume down!

Loud music can damage your ears, so play it quietly.

HANDY EARS

Your ears are useful in more than one way. You use them to help you keep your balance, as well as for hearing.

The outer ear

The ear you see is made of curved cartilage covered in skin. The folds in your ears help to collect sounds and send them into your inner ear.

It takes practice to be good at balancing.

Balance

Your ears also help you balance. Inside your ears are tubes of a liquid that moves about when you move. Nerves in these tubes send messages to your brain. Your brain then sends messages to your muscles to stop you from falling over.

your ear is about as long as your nose.

Hearing problems

Some people have difficulty hearing well. If they cannot hear anything, they are deaf. If they can hear some sounds, they can use a hearing aid. This is a machine that makes sounds louder.

A hearing aid can help people hear talking, music, and other sounds.

TASTE AND SMELL

You taste with your tongue and you smell with your nose. Your sense of smell also helps you taste food.

What is your tongue for?

Your tongue is a muscle. You use it to help you eat, swallow, and speak. It is covered in tiny bumps called taste buds. You have about 10,000 of these. They tell you whether food is sweet, salty, sour, or bitter. Everything you eat is a mixture of these four tastes.

Taste buds like these (seen close up) cover the surface of your tongue.

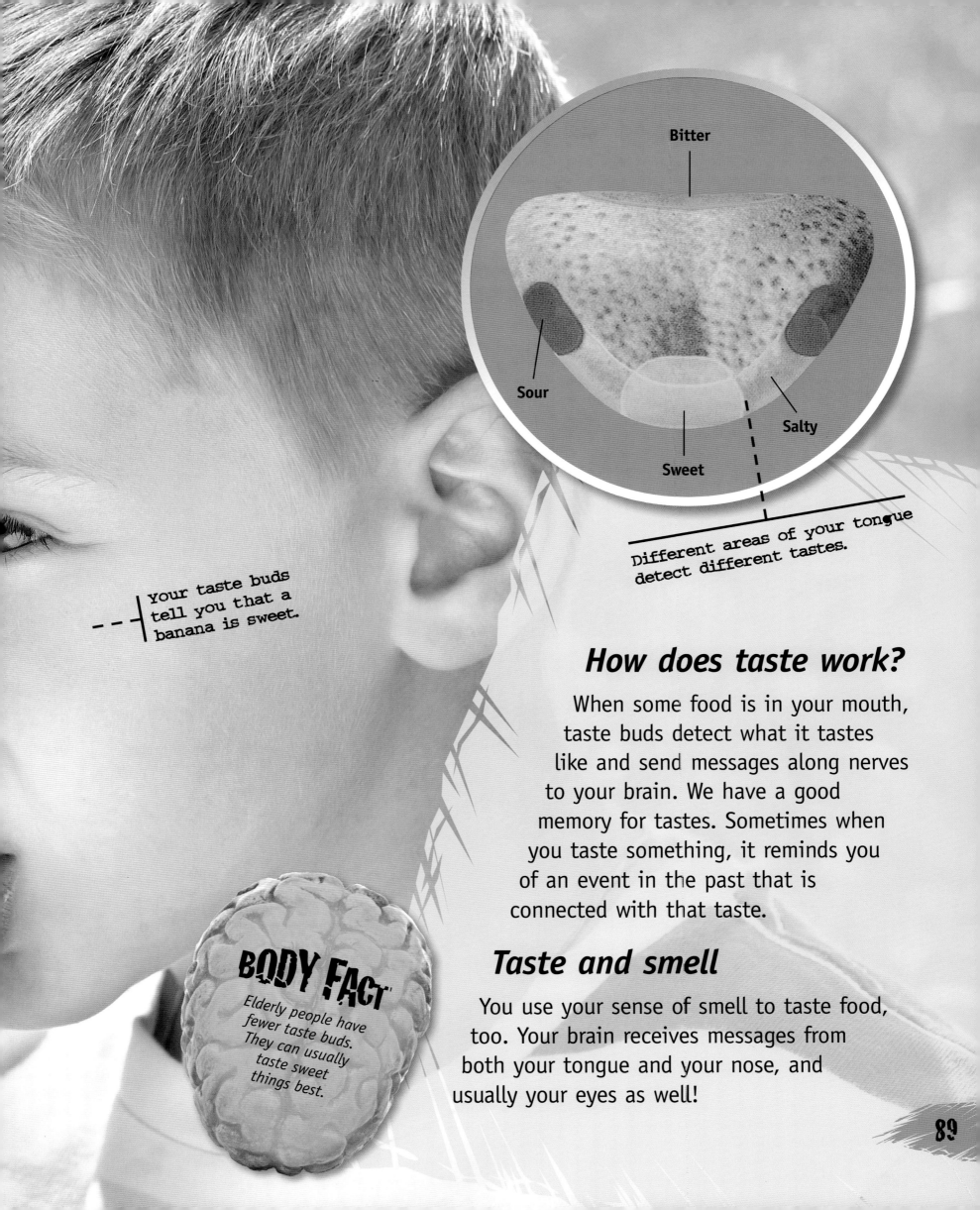

Bitter

Sour

Sweet

Salty

Different areas of your tongue detect different tastes.

Your taste buds tell you that a banana is sweet.

How does taste work?

When some food is in your mouth, taste buds detect what it tastes like and send messages along nerves to your brain. We have a good memory for tastes. Sometimes when you taste something, it reminds you of an event in the past that is connected with that taste.

Taste and smell

You use your sense of smell to taste food, too. Your brain receives messages from both your tongue and your nose, and usually your eyes as well!

BODY FACT

Elderly people have fewer taste buds. They can usually taste sweet things best.

SENSATIONAL SMELLS

Your amazing sense of smell can tell you so much about the world around you. It can give pleasure, warn of danger, and help you taste your food.

How does smell work?

The holes at the end of your nose are your **nostrils**. When you breathe in through your nostrils, your nose warms the air and tiny hairs trap any dust in it. Smelling happens at the top of your nose. The smells in the air are picked up by cells there. They send messages about them along nerves to your brain.

Your brain tells you some smells are lovely.

Noses

Like your ears, your nose is made of cartilage covered in skin. Noses can be many different shapes and sizes, but they all do the same job.

Stuffy nose

When you have a cold, your nose becomes blocked by **mucus**. Then it is much more difficult for your sense of smell to work. Your sense of taste suffers, too. Food tastes much less interesting because you are not smelling it as well.

Food tastes boring when your nose is blocked.

Your brain tells you if a smell is horrible!

YOUR BODY'S BUILDING BLOCKS

Your body is made of millions and millions of tiny cells. Different kinds of cells do different jobs in your body.

Building blocks

Cells are your body's building blocks. You have blood cells, muscle cells, bone cells, nerve cells, fat cells, and many other kinds. Cells can be different shapes and sizes. All cells except red blood cells have a control center called a **nucleus**. This controls what the cells do.

This is a nerve cell. It has long tendrils for sending messages to other nerve cells.

This is a white blood cell. The large pink area is the cell's nucleus.

Tissue

A group of the same kinds of cells collect together to form tissue. For example, a group of muscle cells form muscle tissue. That muscle tissue could be part of an organ, such as your heart.

These long muscle cells are joined together to make muscle tissue.

WHAT MAKES ME, ME?

How you look, how your body works, and many other things about you are decided by instructions in your cells called **genes.**

Genes

Every cell in your body contains instructions, called genes. Genes control what that cell does. Many genes are the same in everyone, while other genes are different. It is the mixture of genes in your cells that makes you different from everyone else.

People in one family share many of the same genes. This is why children, parents, and grandparents often look alike.

Where do genes come from?

You get half of your genes from your mother and half from your father. The way genes are passed on like this is called **inheritance**. If your eyes are the same color as your mother's, you inherited the genes that decide eye color from her. Perhaps you inherited your hair color, or the shape of your nose, from your father.

Genes of diseases

Sometimes genes can make things go wrong in your body. Some diseases or problems are passed from parents to their children in their genes.

The unusual shape of this pupil, or dark area, in the center of this eye is a condition passed in the genes from a parent to a child.

MAKING A BABY

It takes an egg from a woman and a **sperm** from a man to make a baby. The new baby grows inside the mother's body.

Eggs

Every month, a woman's body releases an egg from a part of her body called an **ovary**. It travels along one of her **fallopian tubes** towards the **uterus**, or womb. If it is joined by a sperm that has come from a man's body, the sperm **fertilizes** it. Then it can develop into a new baby.

This sperm is heading towards an egg in order to fertilize it.

Women have two ovaries and two fallopian tubes.

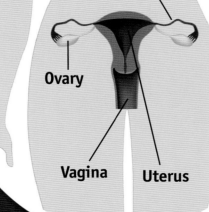

Fallopian tube

Ovary

Vagina　Uterus

Men have two testicles.

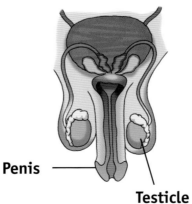

Penis

Testicle

Sperm

A man's sperm develop in a liquid inside his **testicles**. The testicles are connected to the **penis**. Sperm leave his body through the penis.

Identical twins are made when one fertilized egg divides to make two embryos. Both grow into babies in the uterus.

More and more cells

Once the egg is fertilized, it divides into two cells, then four, then eight, and so on. When it reaches the uterus, it stays there and carries on growing. It is now called an **embryo**.

THE DEVELOPING BABY

A woman with a baby growing in her uterus is **pregnant**. It takes about nine months, or forty weeks, for the baby to develop, then it is ready to be born.

Feeding the baby

The developing baby gets food from the mother through a tube called the **umbilical cord.** This tube is connected to the baby at one end and the mother's uterus at the other. Food reaches the baby in blood traveling along the tube.

BODY FACT

Without a baby in it, the uterus is only the size of an apricot! It stretches a lot to hold a growing baby.

It is an exciting time, waiting for a new baby to be born.

Growing fast

After three months, the baby is fully formed, but very tiny. It has arms and legs, fingers and toes, eyes, ears, a nose, and a mouth. It is growing in a sac filled with liquid. It cannot breathe air, but gets oxygen from the mother's blood.

Being pregnant

From about 20 weeks, the mother may feel the baby kicking inside her. As the baby gets bigger, she may feel tired. She has to eat well to feed the developing baby.

At about six weeks after fertilization, the baby is the size of a pea.

The woman's tummy gradually grows as the baby gets bigger. At 40 weeks, the baby is fully grown.

8 weeks   24 weeks   40 weeks

GET READY FOR BIRTH

During the second half of the pregnancy, the baby grows steadily bigger. After nine months, it is ready to be born.

A new body

Slowly, all the parts of the body develop, on the inside and the outside. Babies sleep and wake, suck their thumbs, and even yawn while they are developing.

BODY FACT

Babies are sometimes born early, before 40 weeks. Then they are carefully looked after in the hospital.

The hands start to form at six weeks. They grow tiny nails.

Bigger and bigger

The baby's organs are mostly developed, but it needs to grow bigger. It continues taking oxygen and food from the mother's blood through the umbilical cord. Your belly button is where this cord was attached to you before you were born.

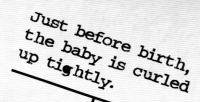

Just before birth, the baby is curled up tightly.

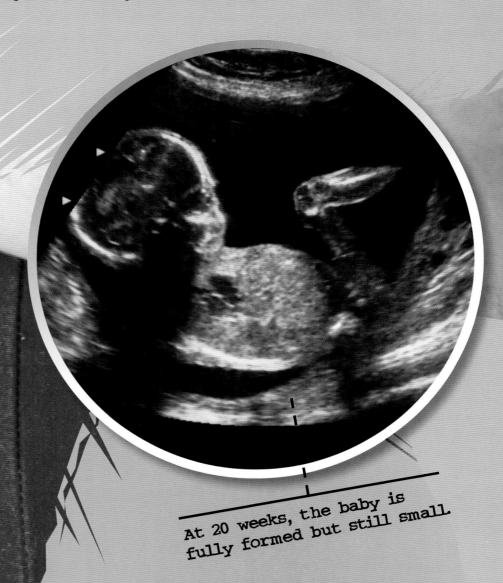

At 20 weeks, the baby is fully formed but still small

Ready for birth

By 40 weeks, the baby's head is upside down—the best position for being born. The baby does not have much room to move. It is curled up tightly. The mother's tummy is very big and heavy. Walking more than a short distance may be uncomfortable for her. When birth begins, muscles in her uterus push the baby out into the world.

GROWING UP

Babies grow very quickly. You grow all through your childhood. You get bigger, and you learn new skills all the time.

Getting moving

Babies cannot move themselves from one place to another. By the time they are one year old, they have learned to sit up and to crawl. They are getting ready to stand up and start walking. By the time they are two, they can run!

This baby has learned to crawl.

Small children learn by playing with simple toys.

Look and learn

Very young children learn about the world around them by using their senses. They look at things, touch them, and put them in their mouths. They learn to pick up objects and to play with them.

Children learn how to tell other people what they want!

Talking

By the age of two, most children can speak a few words. They learn by listening to older children and adults. Slowly, they learn the names of things. They also learn how to play with other children. This prepares them for going to school.

BODY FACT

Babies can only tell us what they want by crying.

BUSY CHILDREN

BODY FACT
During the day, you shrink a little bit as your weight pushes down on your backbone. At night, when you are lying down, your backbone stretches out again.

When you are old enough to go to school, you start to learn even more. You grow bigger, stronger, and wiser!

Going to school

At school, children learn lots of new skills. You learn to read, to write, and all about the world around you. You also learn how to make new friends and get along with people.

Going to school for the first time is a big step in growing up.

It's great when your strong body can give you so much fun!

104

Getting strong

As you get larger, your bones and muscles get stronger. You can control your body and make it work harder. By the age of eight, you can use your body for lots of activities, such as running, dancing, and playing games.

Being creative

Your brain develops as you grow bigger. You have lots of new ideas, so you can make up stories, paint pictures, and make music. Your memory gets better too, so you can remember things from the past.

As you grow older, you can put your creative ideas into action.

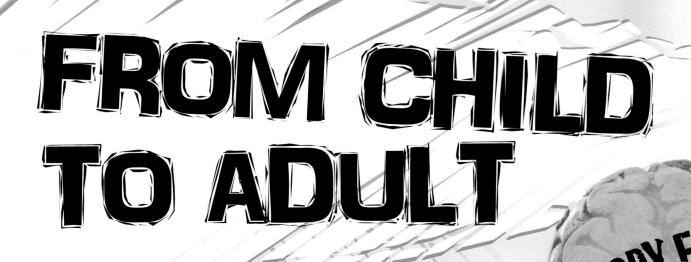

FROM CHILD TO ADULT

From the age of about ten, girls and boys start to become adults. Their bodies change and they become interested in spending more time with each other.

Puberty

The changes that happen in your body as you grow from being a child to an adult are called **puberty**. You grow a lot during the years of puberty. You need more food and more sleep to give you the energy to do this. Puberty usually lasts for four to five years.

Girls

Girls start to develop their adult bodies at a younger age than boys. They grow taller and their breasts start to grow. Their bodies become more rounded in shape. Inside, their bodies are getting ready to have babies.

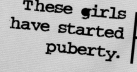

These girls have started puberty.

Boys

A boy's body starts to change at about age 12 or 13. He grows taller and his muscles become stronger. His voice also sounds deeper and his penis grows larger.

Teenage boys grow taller and stronger.

Teenagers need lots of food while they are growing fast.

107

AN EXCITING NEW WORLD

As teenagers grow older, they tend to want to be more independent of their families and to make friends with people of the opposite sex.

What is normal?

There is no fixed age when puberty begins. It is normal for it to begin at any time from the age of 9 or 10 to 15 in girls. For boys, puberty can begin any time from around the age of 12 to 17.

BODY FACT

By the age of about 20, your body has become fully adult. You will not usually grow any taller.

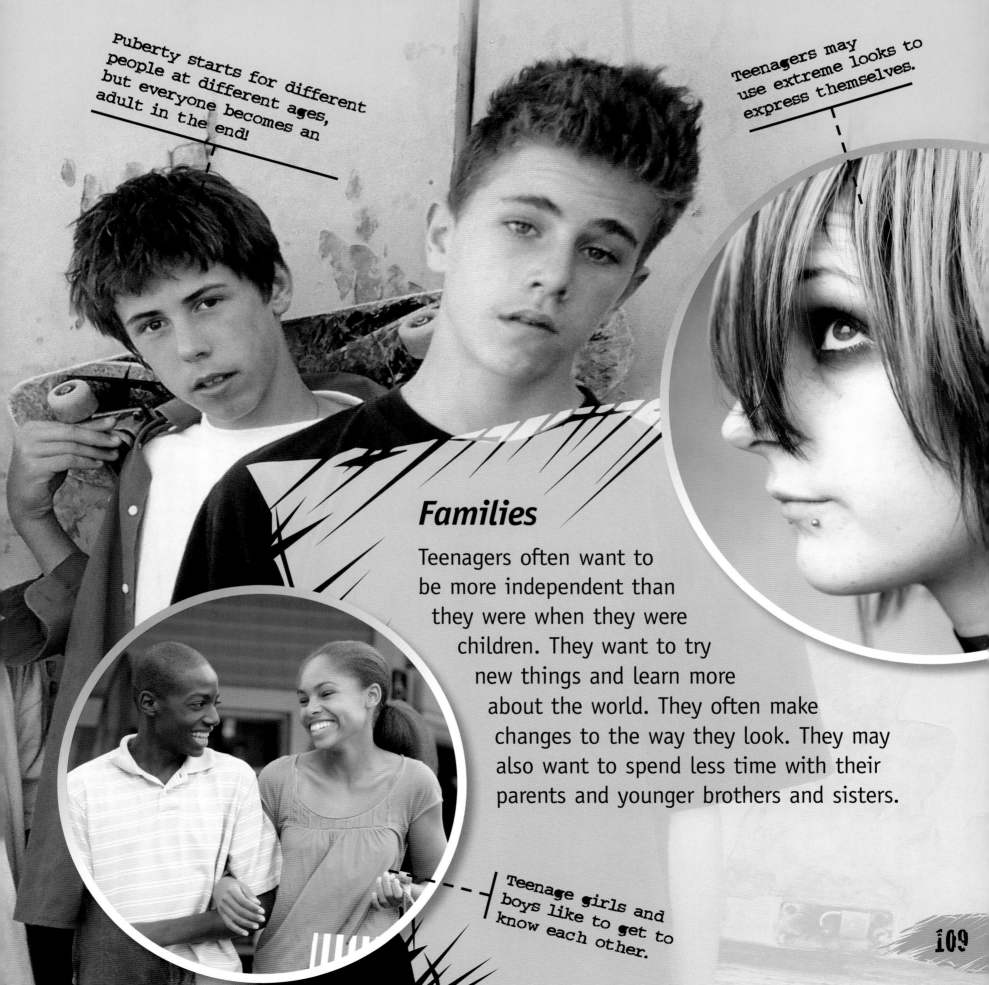

New friendships

As teenagers get older, girls and boys become more interested in going out with each other. They want to develop relationships with people of the opposite sex. Their friends are very important to them, too.

Puberty starts for different people at different ages, but everyone becomes an adult in the end!

Teenagers may use extreme looks to express themselves.

Families

Teenagers often want to be more independent than they were when they were children. They want to try new things and learn more about the world. They often make changes to the way they look. They may also want to spend less time with their parents and younger brothers and sisters.

Teenage girls and boys like to get to know each other.

GETTING OLDER

Your body is strongest when you are in your twenties. As you get older, it is still possible to keep your body fit and healthy for many years.

Strong adults

Over the years, bodies age. Some cells die and are not replaced. Others stop working so well. This happens very slowly. Most people do not notice any difference in how well their body works until they are well past the age of 40, or even older.

Adult bodies can keep working well for many years.

BODY FACT

If your parents and grandparents live until they are very old, you are more likely to live a long time, too.

Raising a family can be shared by more than one generation.

A busy life

Adults have many things to keep them busy. They may work in a job. They may have a family and children to look after. Their bodies are working hard every day.

Slowing down

When people grow older, their bodies change and they have less energy. Their hair becomes gray and their skin becomes wrinkled. They can still enjoy life, but as they become very old, they are more likely to become ill.

People in their 60s and 70s sometimes have more time to enjoy life.

TOO MUCH

It is important to eat enough healthy food each day to keep your body working. However, eating too much food can be bad for you.

Storing energy

You need a certain amount of energy from food every day. We call the energy in food 'calories'. But if you eat too much food, your body cannot use up all the calories in the food. Your body then stores the calories as fat.

Vegetables and fruit do not contain many calories.

BODY FACT

Being very overweight makes it difficult for your heart to pump your blood all round your body.

People who eat too much become overweight and unhealthy.

Not too much sugar and fat

Foods such as cookies, cakes, and chips contain a lot of sugar and fat. Sugar and fat have lots of calories. Eating too much sugar and fat is not good for you and can make you overweight. Try to avoid these foods as much as you can. It is better to choose foods such as bread and pasta when you are hungry. These foods fill you up and give you lots of energy.

Foods such as cakes and biscuits contain a lot of calories.

TOO LITTLE

It is important to eat enough food. Your body and brain need the energy you get from food to move and to concentrate.

Energy from food

To make sure you have enough energy, try to eat lots of energy-giving foods such as brown bread and rice. Fruits such as dates, figs, raisins, and bananas will also help to feed your body with the energy it needs.

BODY FACT
You need to eat lots of different kinds of food every day to keep your body healthy.

Bananas are a great energy-giving food.

Not enough

It is important not to eat too little. You need to eat enough food to make sure your body will work properly. If you do not eat enough protein every day, your muscles will not grow. Your skin and nails will start to look unhealthy, too. You need to eat food for vitamins and minerals. These keep your body healthy. Without them, you may become ill.

A healthy snack of raisins or dates gives your body lots of energy.

If you do not eat enough of the right things, you may start to catch illnesses, such as colds.

FOOD HYGIENE

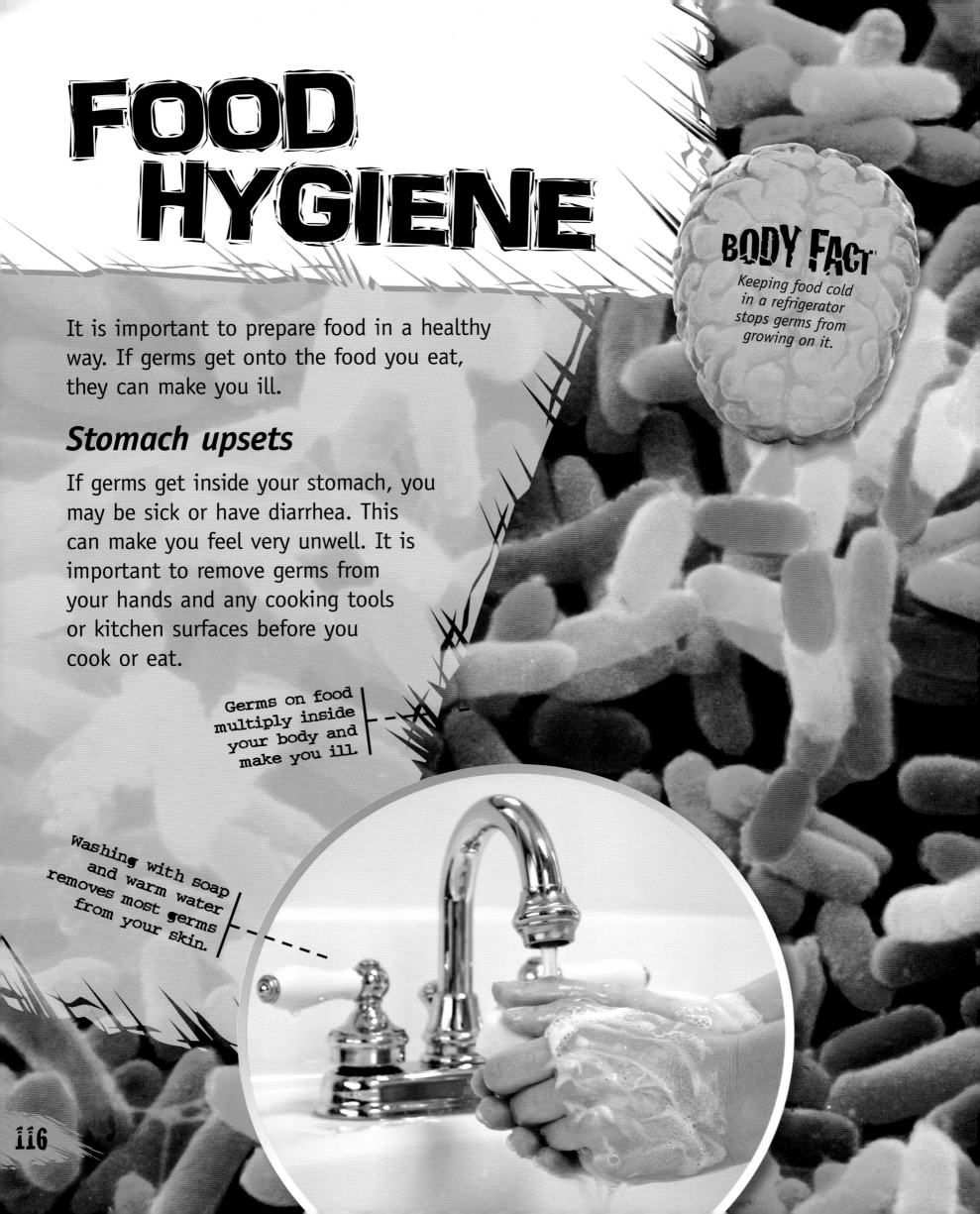

It is important to prepare food in a healthy way. If germs get onto the food you eat, they can make you ill.

Stomach upsets

If germs get inside your stomach, you may be sick or have diarrhea. This can make you feel very unwell. It is important to remove germs from your hands and any cooking tools or kitchen surfaces before you cook or eat.

Germs on food multiply inside your body and make you ill

Washing with soap and warm water removes most germs from your skin.

Germs on skin

Some germs live on the skin, which is why it is important to wash your hands with soap and warm water before you touch any food or begin to cook. Always wash your hands after using the bathroom and before you eat.

Use your eyes and nose to check whether food has gone bad

Bad food

Do not eat food that has become moldy or has passed its sell-by date. Once food has gone bad, it can contain bacteria that will make you sick.

GET BUSY!

To keep your body healthy, you need to stay active.

Get going!

Your body is built for use, so use it! Get lots of exercise. Play sports or games with your friends and family. For short journeys, ask adults if you can walk or cycle instead of going by car, if it is safe. Go outside to play as often as you can.

Warm up those muscles before you get really active.

BODY FACT
Keeping your muscles flexible by gently stretching them is especially important while you are growing rapidly.

Exercise safely

Before you exercise, it is important to make sure your body is ready to work. If you do not prepare your body to exercise, you might pull a muscle. Warm up your muscles before exercising by walking or moving slowly. Gently stretch your muscles by touching your toes or stretching your arms above your head.

Exercise can bring people together.

Winding down

It's a good idea to stretch after you have finished exercising, too. This helps your muscles to cool and relax.

Gently stretch your muscles again after vigorous exercise.

EXERCISE IS FUN

There are lots of different exercises you can choose to do. It's always possible to find some kind of exercise or sport that you like.

Exercises for every part of you

Different types of exercise are good for different parts of your body. Some exercises, such as running and riding a bicycle, are healthy for your heart and lungs. If you feel a little out of breath when you exercise, this shows that your heart and lungs are working hard to push blood and oxygen around your body. Running and cycling also make your muscles work harder.

BODY FACT
Exercise doesn't have to be sports. Playing on playground equipment is great exercise too.

Cycling fast makes your heart and lungs work harder.

Muscle strength

Exercise that includes jumping and pushing works your muscles hard. When you do a handstand or a cartwheel, you make the muscles in your arms work hard. When you jump off a wall onto the ground, the muscles in your legs work hard.

Get together

There are lots of ways to have fun while you exercise. If you like playing with friends, why not try a team sport such as football or netball? If you like water, try swimming. If you love music, dancing is great exercise.

Ballet gives your muscles a workout.

GETTING REST

You need plenty of exercise, but you need to get enough rest too. Your body mends itself when you rest, to be ready to work hard again the next day.

Time for bed

Children need 10 to 12 hours of sleep every night to stay healthy. When you are asleep, your body repairs any damage to it that may have happened during the day. This is the time when bruises, bumps, and cuts mend and heal.

Resting allows your body's healing system to get to work.

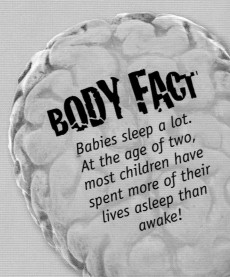

BODY FACT
Babies sleep a lot. At the age of two, most children have spent more of their lives asleep than awake!

A bedtime routine

To make sure you get enough sleep, try to go to bed at the same time every night. This will help your body to get into a good routine. Avoid watching television just before you go to sleep. Instead, allow your mind to slow down by reading a book or having a warm bath.

Reading relaxes you before you go to sleep.

Sweet dreams!

Essential sleep

If you do not get enough sleep, you will find it hard to concentrate during the day. You will also find it hard to exercise and to have fun with your friends. Learn to love your sleep!

LOOK AFTER YOUR SKIN

Your skin is precious. It protects you from harm and keeps you warm. You need to keep it in good condition, to last you all your life.

Keep covered

You probably don't think much about your skin—until you cut or bruise it. But you need to protect it from damage. The Sun's powerful rays can do a lot of harm to your skin. When you are outside on a sunny day, cover up as much as possible with loose clothes, and put sunscreen on the exposed parts of your skin.

If your toenails grow too long, they can damage the skin on your toes.

Hands and feet

You can protect the skin on your hands and feet by keeping your nails in good condition. Cut them before they grow too long.

Keep clean

Germs live on your skin, so get rid of them by washing regularly with soap. If you get a cut, make sure you clean out any dirt in it, and cover it with a bandage until it starts to heal.

During puberty, teenagers are likely to have breakouts of pimples on their skins. Therefore it's extra important they keep their skins clean.

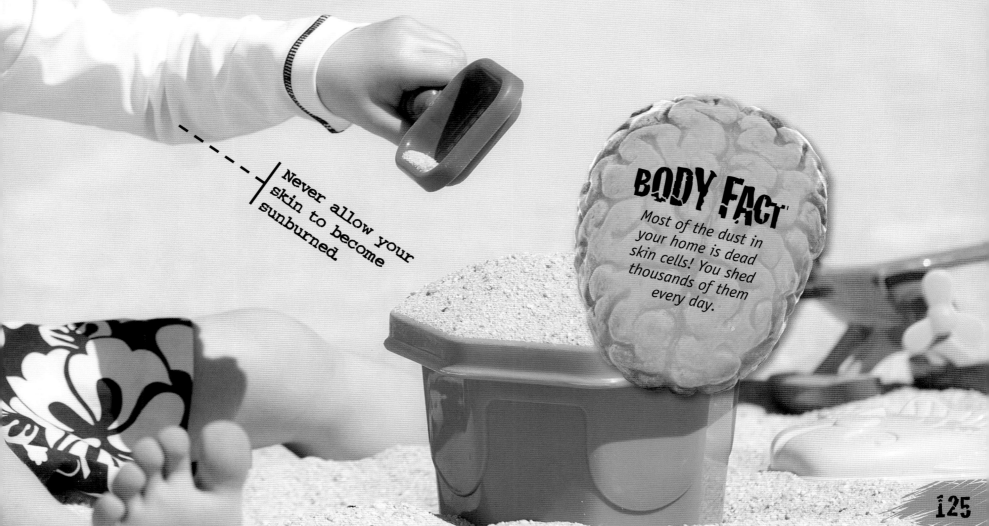

Never allow your skin to become sunburned

BODY FACT
Most of the dust in your home is dead skin cells! You shed thousands of them every day.

LOOK AFTER YOUR HAIR

Your hair keeps you warm and looks great, but it's important to keep it healthy, too.

Long or short?

Hair comes in so many different colors and styles. Is your hair curly, wavy, or straight? Do you like it to be long or short? Whatever you choose, keep your hair clean by washing it every few days. This will keep dirt and other particles out of it and stop it from becoming tangled.

A new haircut can make you feel great. It's fun to try new styles.

BODY FACT

Your hair grows faster in summer than it does in winter. It also grows more during the day than at night.

Brushing your hair keeps it in good condition and looking fantastic, too!

Tie long hair back to keep it out of harm's way.

Safety

If you are doing something that could damage your hair, keep it out of the way. Keep it away from flames, for example, and from fast-moving machinery such as fans.

Cut it

It's a good idea to have your hair cut regularly. Hairs sometimes become weak at the ends and then split. If you love having long hair, you can help keep it strong by cutting off these ends. Using a hot-air hairdryer will also damage your hair, so let it dry naturally.

BANISH HEAD LICE!

Children often get lice in their hair. They are not dirty or a sign of bad hygiene, but it's a good idea to get rid of them.

Nasty nits

Nits are the egg shells of tiny insects called head lice. The lice cling to hairs and feed off blood from your scalp. You may not notice you have them. Your head may only feel itchy. Head lice are passed from one head to another when in close contact, for example when you work closely with someone in a classroom.

Head lice love living in clean hair.

BODY FACT
Head lice can only live on human hair. They don't live in soft furnishings or bedding.

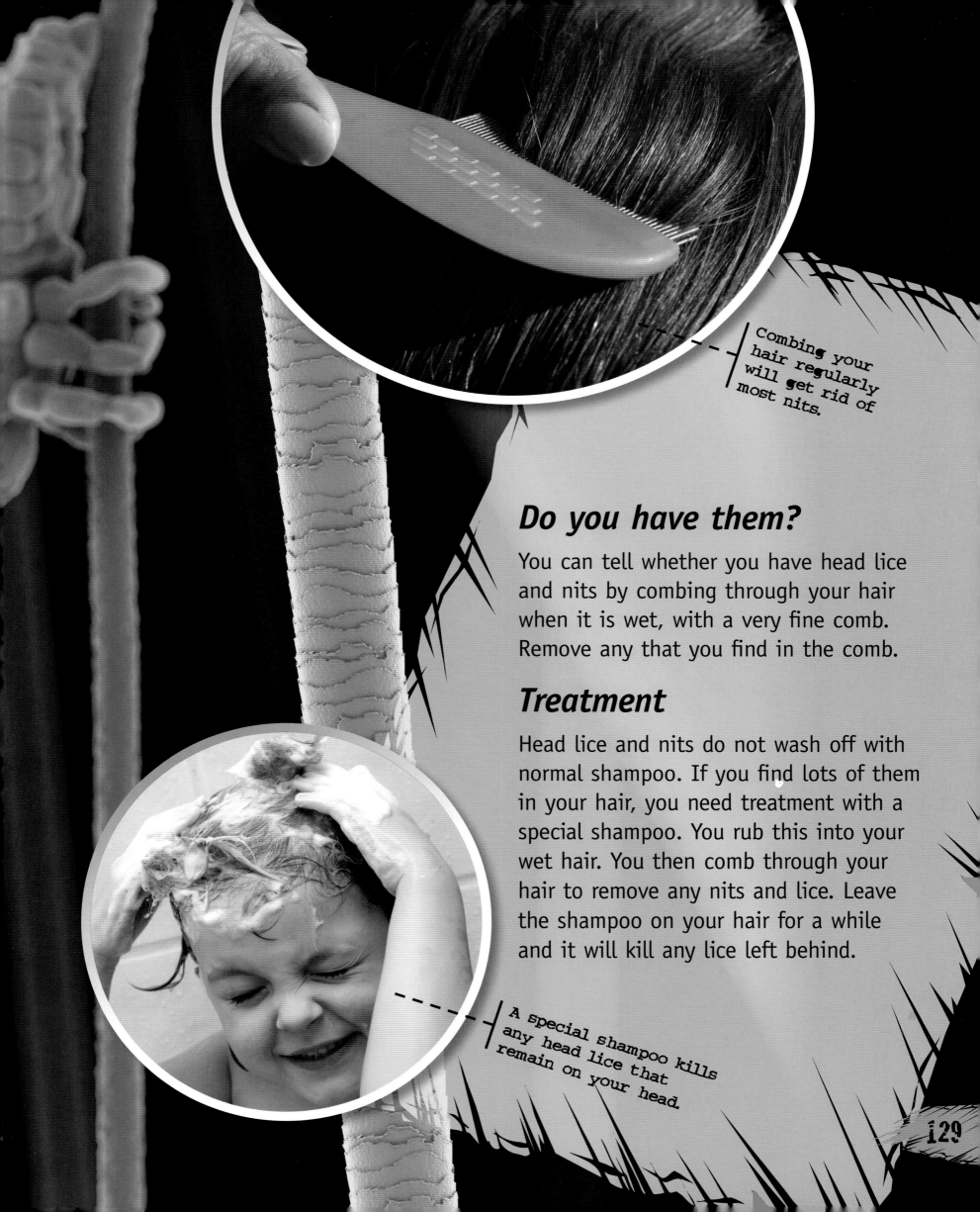

Combing your hair regularly will get rid of most nits.

Do you have them?

You can tell whether you have head lice and nits by combing through your hair when it is wet, with a very fine comb. Remove any that you find in the comb.

Treatment

Head lice and nits do not wash off with normal shampoo. If you find lots of them in your hair, you need treatment with a special shampoo. You rub this into your wet hair. You then comb through your hair to remove any nits and lice. Leave the shampoo on your hair for a while and it will kill any lice left behind.

A special shampoo kills any head lice that remain on your head

TREASURE YOUR TEETH!

Your second set of teeth must last you a lifetime. Develop good habits to keep them healthy.

If you do not clean your teeth, they can become stained.

Tooth decay

Tooth decay happens when holes appear in teeth's hard outside enamel layer. Sugary foods can wear away the enamel and make holes in it. Avoid having too many sugary foods and drinks. The sugar stays on your teeth and begins to eat them away.

BODY FACT
Do not brush your teeth too hard—it can damage your gums.

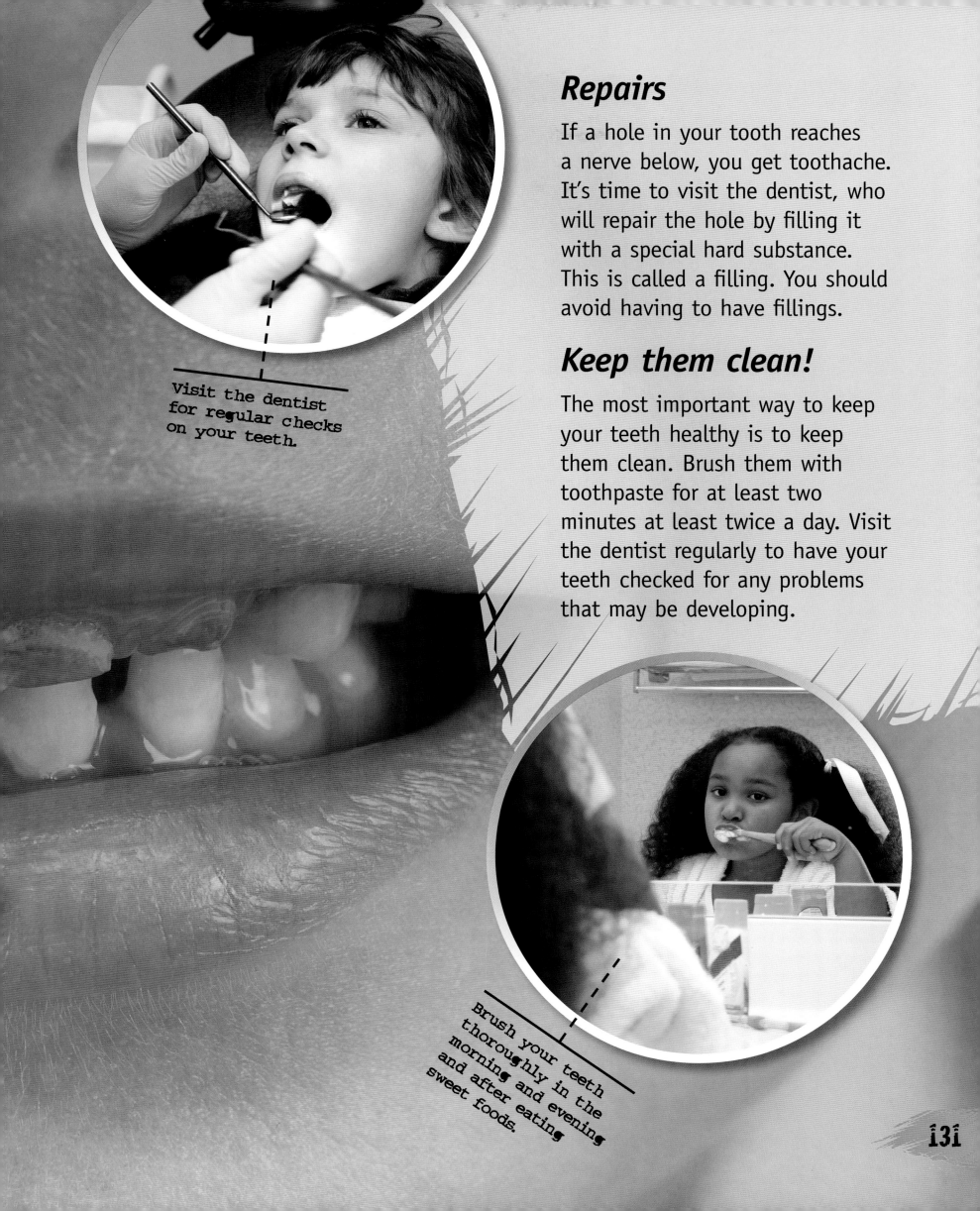

Repairs

If a hole in your tooth reaches a nerve below, you get toothache. It's time to visit the dentist, who will repair the hole by filling it with a special hard substance. This is called a filling. You should avoid having to have fillings.

Keep them clean!

The most important way to keep your teeth healthy is to keep them clean. Brush them with toothpaste for at least two minutes at least twice a day. Visit the dentist regularly to have your teeth checked for any problems that may be developing.

Visit the dentist for regular checks on your teeth.

Brush your teeth thoroughly in the morning and evening and after eating sweet foods.

PROTECT YOUR HEARING

You cannot replace your ears if they are damaged, so treat them well.

Hear this

The inside of your ear is very delicate. This is why your hearing is so good. You can hear the quietest sounds, from far away, and tell what they are. It's important not to damage the inside of your ears. Never put anything into them, even a finger. Do not clean them with a cotton bud, as this can damage the tiny hairs inside, and even the eardrum.

your inner ear can easily be damaged, so do not touch it.

132

Protect your ears from very loud noises.

Wax

If you think your ears are full of sticky wax that is making it difficult for you to hear, you should see a doctor. They can remove the wax safely, without damaging your hearing. Do not pick at it yourself.

Turn it down!

Your hearing can also be affected by very loud noises. People who listen to loud music on headphones for a long time can seriously damage their hearing. People who work with loud machinery wear protection over their ears. If you like listening to music, keep the volume down.

LOOK AFTER YOUR NOSE!

Your nose is important! It helps you breathe in and sense smells around you. Your nose also stops dirt and germs from getting inside your body.

Don't pick it!

Just like your ears, eyes, and skin, it is important to keep your nose clean. This will stop unwanted germs from getting into your body. Avoid picking your nose. When you do this, you transfer germs onto your fingers. If you then touch food without washing your hands, the germs can get inside your body. Blow your nose with a tissue instead.

BODY FACT
It is traditional for the Maori people in New Zealand to greet each other by pressing their noses together.

Inuit people also greet each other by rubbing noses.

Blow germs and mucus out of your nose and into a tissue.

Blocked!

When you have a cold, your nose makes extra mucus to soak up the germs. Blow your nose with a tissue to get rid of the mucus, then put the tissue in a bin with a lid. This will stop the germs being passed on to another person.

HAPPY AND HEALTHY

What makes us happy? If you look after your body, eat well, exercise, and have fun with other people, it's easy to be happy.

Get moving

When you exercise, your body releases chemicals that make you feel happy. These chemicals also make you feel more relaxed, which helps you rest. Try going for a run or a cycle ride and see how you feel afterwards. Do you feel happier and full of energy?

Exercise makes you feel good.

Drinking milk shortly before bedtime can help you get to sleep.

Good mood food

Healthy foods feed your body with the vitamins and minerals it needs to keep you feeling happy, too. Some foods contain special chemicals that help to make you feel happy. Bananas, milk, and peanuts all contain a chemical called tryptophan which makes you feel good and helps you get to sleep.

Share your worries

Everyone has worries sometimes. It's a really good idea to talk about them with someone you trust, such as a good friend or family member. They will listen, and help you deal with them.

Sharing your worries with other people often makes them seem less worrying.

137

GLOSSARY

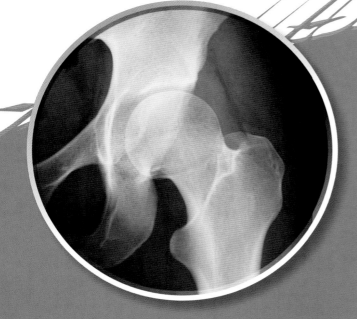

Arteries
A blood vessel that carries blood away from your heart.

Bacteria
Germs made of just one cell. Some bacteria cause diseases.

Bladder
The place where urine is stored in your body before you go to the toilet.

Blood vessels
Tubes that carry blood all around your body.

Bone marrow
A soft substance inside some bones, where new blood is made.

Braille
The system of reading through touch used by the blind.

Brain
The organ in your head that controls all the workings of your body.

Calcium
A substance found in milk and cheese that helps your bones grow strong.

Carbohydrates
A substance found in some foods that gives you lots of energy.

Carbon dioxide
A gas found in air. We breathe out carbon dioxide that we do not want.

Cartilage
A substance your nose and ears are made of that can bend. Cartilage also surrounds the ends of bones at the joints, so that they can move smoothly over each other.

Cells
The building blocks of the body and all living things.

Circulation
The movement of blood through your heart and around your body.

Decibels
The units used to measure sound.

Dentine
A substance in your teeth under the outside layer of enamel.

Dermis
The second layer of your skin, under the epidermis.

Diaphragm
A muscle in your chest that is connected to your rib bones. It tightens when you breathe in and relaxes when you breathe out.

Digestion
The process of breaking down food, getting the goodness out of it, and getting rid of any waste that is left over.

Digestive system
The organs in your body that work together to make digestion happen.

Eardrum
A small, thin piece of tissue stretched tight inside your ear. It vibrates when sounds reach it, so that you hear.

Embryo
The name for the early stage of a new baby developing inside a mother's uterus.

Enamel
A very hard layer that covers the part of your teeth above your gums.

Epidermis
The outside layer of your skin, made mostly of dead skin cells.

Fallopian tubes
Two tubes inside a woman's body that join the ovaries to the uterus.

Fertilization
The process of a man's sperm joining with a woman's egg to start the development of a new baby.

Genes
Instructions in every cell of your body that tell it what to do.

Hemoglobin
A substance that carries oxygen around your body via the blood.

Heart
The muscle in your chest that beats to pump blood through your body.

Infection
Invasion of germs, such as bacteria or viruses, that get into your body and cause damage or harm.

Inheritance
The instructions you receive from the genes of your parents that affect what you look like.

Iris
The colored part of your eye.

Joint
A place in the body where bones meet and are joined, so that you can move.

Keratin
The main protein substance that makes your hair and nails.

Kidneys
The two organs in your body that clean waste materials from your blood.

Large intestine
The last part of your digestive system, where some water is taken out and waste collects.

Lens
The part of your eye that makes a picture of what you see.

Ligaments
Bands of fibers that stretch and join muscles to bones.

Lungs
The two organs in your body through which oxygen in the air you breathe passes into your blood.

Milk teeth
The first set of teeth that a child grows. Milk teeth fall out during childhood and are replaced by adult teeth.

GLOSSARY

Minerals
Substances found in food that help your body work well.

Mucus
Slime produced by the body to protect itself.

Muscles
Bundles of fibers that tighten and relax to make parts of your body move.

Nervous system
The network of nerves that carry messages to and from your brain.

Nostrils
The two holes at the end of your nose.

Nucleus
The central part of a cell.

Nutrients
The goodness in food that your body needs to work.

Optical illusion
The experience of seeing something differently to what it actually is.

Organs
The parts of your body that have a particular job to do. Your heart, brain, skin, stomach, liver, and kidneys are all organs.

Ovaries
The two places in a woman's body where eggs are stored.

Oxygen
A gas in the air that your body needs to stay alive.

Penis
A man passes urine through his penis. Sperm also leave the body through the penis.

Plasma
A colorless liquid in blood that makes it runny.

Pores
Tiny holes in your skin. Sweat comes out through your pores.

Pregnant
A woman is pregnant when a baby is developing inside her body.

Proteins
Substances found in food that help your body grow.

Puberty
The years when boys and girls start to become adults who can reproduce.

Pupil
The black circle at the center of your eye. It is a hole that lets light into your eye.

Rectum
The last part of the large intestine.

Red blood cells
The cells in blood that carry oxygen to all parts of your body.

Retina
The place at the back of the eye that receives the picture from the lens.

Saliva
A liquid produced in your mouth that starts to break down food.

Senses
You have five senses to tell you about the world around you: sight, hearing, taste, smell, and touch.

Skeleton
The framework of your entire body, made of bones.

Small intestine
The part of the digestive system where food goes when it leaves your stomach. Most of the goodness in food is taken into your blood here.

Sperm
The cell produced by a man that joins with a woman's egg to fertilize it.

Spinal cord
The longest cord in the body's nervous system, running from your head to your bottom.

Spine
The backbone.

Taste buds
Tiny lumps on the surface of your tongue that can detect the tastes sweet, sour, bitter, and salty.

Testicles
The two sacs on the outside of a man's body where sperm are stored.

Tissue
Material produced when cells of the same kind join together, such as skin tissue and muscle tissue.

Umbilical cord
A tube that joins a developing baby to the mother, inside the uterus.

Urine
The body's liquid waste product: pee.

Uterus
The place inside a mother's body where a new baby develops; also called the womb.

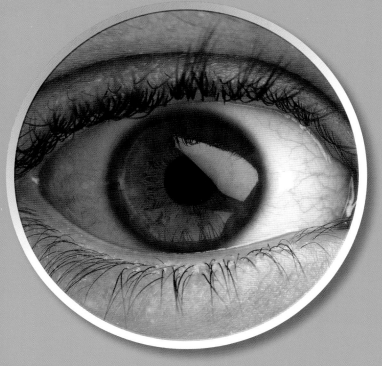

Veins
Blood vessels that carry blood from the body back to the heart.

Viruses
Germs made from just one molecule that can cause diseases.

Vitamins
Substances found in food that help your body work well.

White blood cells
Cells in your blood that fight and destroy germs.

X-ray
A photograph of the inside of your body.

INDEX

Sandy Creek
NEW YORK

An Imprint of Sterling Publishing
387 Park Avenue South
New York, NY 10016

Design and Editorial: Calcium

ISBN: 978-1-4351-4407-1 (print format)

A CIP record for this book is available from the Library of Congress.

For information about custom editions, special sales, and premium and corporate purchases, please contact Sterling Special Sales at 800-805-5489 or specialsales@sterlingpublishing.com.

Manufactured in China
Lot #:
2 4 6 8 10 9 7 5 3 1
09/12

Picture credits
Key: t = top, b = bottom, c = center, l = left, r = right

Alamy 79tr Sinibomb Images, 134br Alaska Stock
Corbis 124br STUDIO TEC/a.collectionRF/amanaimages
Dreamstime 126–127 Hallgerd
Getty Images 15bc Steve Gschmeissner, 16 Science Photo Library, 27 Visuals Unlimited, Inc./Dr. Fred Hossler, 30bl Alain Pol, ISM, 33cl Dr. Richard Kessel & Dr. Gene Shih, 36 MoMo Productions, 41 Visuals Unlimited, Inc./Anne Weston/Cancer Research UK, 43tr David Tipling, 48bc Visuals Unlimited, Inc./Dr. Volker Brinkmann, 49bc AFP, 53bl Coneyl Jay, 59 CNRI, 64–65 Thomas Deernick, NCMIR, 64tr Medical Images, 93br Ed Reschke, 128–129 Science Picture Co., 129tc Charles Bowman
Istockphoto 45bl Sarah Musselman, 47tl Don Bayley, 53tr Stephan Zabel
Science Photo Library 10bl David Scharf, 13bc Susumu Nishinaga, 25bc Du Cane Medical Imaging Ltd, 34 Tony Mcconnell, 42 Dr Fred Hossler/Visuals Unlimited, Inc, 44 David Scharf, 45tc Adam Hart-Davis, 58 Manfred Kage, 66–67 Dr Keith Wheeler, 66 Carol & Mike Werner/Visuals Unlimited,Inc, 73c James Cavallini, 76c Manfred Kage, 88bc Biophoto Associates, 93br Michael Abbey, 99tl Endelmann, 100bc Neil Bromhall/Genesis Films, 116–117 NIBSC
Shutterstock 4–5 Mat Hayward, 5bc Konstantin Yolshin, 5tl Melianiaka Kanstantsin, 6–7 Cheryl Casey, 8bl Tyler Olson, 8–9 Golden Pixels LLC, 9br Anette Linnea Rasmussen, 10–11 Monkey Business Images, 11br Blend Images, 12–13 illustrart, 13cr SerrNovik, 14–15 photomak, 14r aquatic creature, 17bl Goodluz, 17tr zirconicusso, 18 Zurijeta, 20 Dmitriy Shironosov, 21bc botazsolti, 21tr Monkey Business Images, 22–23 Lisa S., 23cr deckard_73, 24 bikeriderlondon, 25tr Oleg Kozlov, 28–29 Laura Stone, 29tr Karen Struthers, 30–31 Mandy Godbehear, 31cr Daisy Daisy, 32–33 Andreas Matzke, 35 Charles Knowles, 37 Sebastian Kaulitzki, 38 Digital Media Pro, 39bc Alexander Raths, 39tr wavebreakmedia ltd, 40 mehmetcan, 43bl Suzanne Tucker, 46 Arvind Balaraman, 47br PedroVieira, 48 Fedor Kondratenko, 51 eAlisa, 55bc spotmatik, 55tc Monkey Business Images, 56 monticello, 56bc JMiks, 57br jreika, 60 BestPhotoStudio, 61tr Joerg Beuge, 62 paulaphoto, 64bc tlorna, 68–69 Peter Bernik, 69br Juriah Mosin, 70br Forster Forest, 71tr CREATISTA, 72–73 Ami Parikh, 72bl Juriah Mosin, 74–75 AISPIX by Image Source, 74br Martin Novak, 75cr Paul Maguire, 77l Velychko, 77tr Xiaojiao Wang, 78 originalpunkt, 79 Pietus, 79bl Alsu, 80–81 olly, 80bl Dragana Gerasimoski, 81br P√©ter Gudella, 82–83 Carlos Caetano, 82br Aaron Amat, 83tr, AISPIX by Image Source, 84–85 wavebreakmedia ltd, 85cr Zherui WU, 86 AISPIX by Image Source, 87bl Paul Matthew Photography, 87tr Andre Blais, 88–89 Maxim Blinkov, 90–91 zhuda, 91cr Monkey Business Images, 91tl Gelpi, 92–93 Sebastian Kaulitzki, 94–95 Monkey Business Images, 94br Monkey Business Images, 95bl Shvaygert Ekaterina, 96–97 Sebastian Kaulitzki, 97cr AISPIX by Image Source, 98 S.Borisov, 101 Suzanne Tucker, 102–103 AISPIX by Image Source, 102bl Poznyakov, 103tc Karen Struthers, 104–105 Mat Hayward, 104bc Morgan Lane Photography, 105cr Juriah Mosin, 106–107 Monkey Business Images, 106br Monkey Business Images, 107cr Jamie Roach, 108–109 AISPIX by Image Source, 109bl Monkey Business Images, 109cr CREATISTA, 110 lightpoet, 111tl CandyBox Images, 111br PT Images, 112–113 Kiselev Andrey Valerevich, 113bl MSPhotographic, 113tr SVLuma, 114–115 Marcio Jose Bastos Silva, 115br Poznyakov, 115tl f9photos, 116bc Elena Elisseeva, 117cr CCat82, 118–119 Monkey Business Images, 118bl samotrebizan, 119bl Marcia Crayton, 120–121 Monkey Business Images, 121br Ann Worthy, 122–123 Katrina Brown, 123tr artur gabrysiak, 123br kRie, 124–125 Aleksei Potov, 125tr Jorg Hackemann, 126bl Levent Konuk, 127tr auremar, 129bl Renata Osinska, 130–131 Levent Konuk, 131br Jaimie Duplass, 131tc Dmitry Kalinovsky, 132–133 olly, 133tc Losevsky Photo and Video, 134–135 llaszlo, 136–137 Studio1One, 136br Alena Ozerova, 137 Rob Marmion.